1964

kept

HOW TO STUDY IN COLLEGE

HOW TO

STUDY IN

COLLEGE

605

WALTER PAUK · DIRECTOR, READING-STUDY CENTER
CORNELL UNIVERSITY

HOUGHTON MIFFLIN COMPANY · **BOSTON**
NEW YORK · ATLANTA · GENEVA, ILL. · DALLAS · PALO ALTO

Contents

Preface

Nine years' experience at the Cornell Reading-Study Center has convinced me that any student who wants to be helped can be helped. Time and again students have told me that by learning a particular technique for taking notes, remembering what they read, or attacking a difficult subject such as mathematics or one of the sciences, they have achieved a major breakthrough. Moreover, it not infrequently happens that improvement in a few study techniques opens the door to solution of a whole complex of related though more deep-lying problems.

Such students are not primarily interested in theory, and most of them have little patience with merely inspirational talk. What they mainly want is simple, practical instruction on how to tackle and overcome their special difficulties. They want something they can readily understand and apply, and something that works. This book stresses practical study techniques which, in my experience with thousands of students, have been found to work.

These techniques are the product of extensive trial and experiment based on the most widely tested educational and learning theory. But the tail is never allowed to wag the dog. While theory is always implicit, and is sometimes given in enough detail to assure the skeptic or explain the rationale of a recommended technique, it is never presented without explicit instruction on how to apply it, and it is never used simply as exhortation. After all, the person who needs penicillin is seldom cured by learning the history of antibiotics.

The chief method of this book, then, is to translate theory and the findings of research into specific tools which a student can grasp and use. In attempting to make the book concrete I have relied heavily on visual examples. The student is shown economical ways of scheduling his time. He is shown facsimiles of lecture notes and the relative advantages and disadvantages of various methods of note-taking. He is shown how topic sentences and transitional expressions summarize an idea and relate the parts of a discussion. He is shown how and how not to mark the books he studies, to take notes on his reading, and to answer questions on an examination. He thus learns by vivid example to apply the precepts which research in learning and education has led us to.

Among these precepts is the importance of attitudes in successful learning, both as a factor in the original motivation to improve, and as a product of improvement. Some students seek help through a genuine desire to do better, but many are driven to do so by fear of what may happen to them if they don't. But whatever the drive to begin with, few can resist the lift of spirit and the deep sense of satisfaction that is the natural reward of success. And few can fail to be strengthened in favorable attitudes toward study by the mere fact of having done it well and honestly enough not only to pass examinations, but to retain their newly acquired knowledge so that it provides a solid foundation for more. For this reason I am wholeheartedly against tricks and gimmicks which overnight can fill the mind with "knowledge" which melts away after the examination and leaves all to be done over again.

A word should be said before I close in thanks to the persons who have contributed to or written the last six chapters, those on the study of special subjects and on mental health. I am deeply indebted to the following: to Mr. Ian D. Elliot of Ithaca for the chapter on writing themes and course papers; to Mr. James A. Wood of Cornell University for the chapter on speeches and oral reports; to Professor William G. Moulton of Princeton University for permission to reprint the chapter on study hints for students of foreign languages; to Professors Walter B. Carver and Harrison A. Geiselmann of Cornell University for their contributions to the chapter on the study of mathematics; to Professor Kenneth Greisen of Cornell University for his contribution to the chapter on the study of the sciences; to Professor Benjamin S. Bloom and Miss Lois J. Brodner for valuable ideas on the techniques of problem-solving; to Dr. George S. Stevenson and Mr. Harry Milt of The National Association for Mental Health, Inc., for permission to reprint the chapter on living realistically. Finally I am eternally grateful to my many students of the Cornell Reading-Study Center who have taught me so much, that I may pass a little on to others.

WALTER PAUK

1

Setting Your Sights

Ponce de Leon scoured the swamps of Florida for a "fountain of youth" which he must at times have known did not exist. Similarly, thousands of students seek an easy road to success in college. Those who are looking for a magic formula to good grades — either in this book or elsewhere — will be disappointed. They are likely to graduate virtually uneducated and near the bottom of their class, if indeed they graduate at all.

THREE INGREDIENTS FOR SUCCESS

Trite as it may sound, there are three basic ingredients in the make-up of most successful college students. These are intelligence above the average; the ability to work constructively; and the will to succeed, to get the most out of one's academic opportunities.

Intelligence. Since colleges are continually raising standards, and competition to get in is ever more intense, the mere fact that the student is in college presupposes a certain native intelligence. This, however, is rarely enough by itself, and it can be fatal to assume that because one did well in high school, he needn't work hard now. Almost every college student did well in high school.

The point is that students bright enough to get top grades in high school with little effort are easily lulled into believing that they can do the same in college. They can't. This is a mistake from which a surprising number of freshmen never recover, with the unhappy result that they are forced to drop out of college by the end of the first year.

The usual story goes like this: At mid-term the student is shocked by the low grades he gets. So he tries harder, but finds in despair that he did not develop good study habits in high school, and even though he works hard his grades don't improve much. Repeated low grades shake his confidence; resentment mounts with desperation; and the end is inevitable — academic failure, humiliation, and a bitter sense of defeat.

Ability to work constructively. Intelligence is indispensable, but so is the second of our three ingredients, the ability to work constructively. Indeed, this ability often means the difference between a passing and a failing grade. On it rest the mechanics of college study, which like any mechanics can be improved by practice in the observance of certain general rules. This book shows efficient ways of doing many of the mechanical things connected with study, such as reading textbooks, taking lecture notes, reviewing for examinations, and studying specific subjects.

Working constructively is a very different thing from merely working hard. Most of us have seen an inexperienced driver vainly try to coax a car out of a mudhole or up a snowy slope. He spins the wheels until the tires smoke, yet makes no progress. This is undirected effort, resulting only in waste of gas, tires, and time. Should he redirect his effort by spreading sand under the tires, or prepare for trouble by having chains or snowtires, the car could move slowly but steadily toward safer ground. In the same way, time and energy can easily be wasted in inefficient study, but the same time and energy, directed systematically and intelligently, can lead to gratifying results.

Inefficient study methods have an impact even upon able students who, though their grades may be fairly good, express frustration over getting so little learning for so much effort. They feel they are being short-changed educationally.

Effective study methods can be learned and made habitual. One's college life should be run systematically, just as any job or profession is run. Almost every successful student I have talked to reported that it was only when he scheduled his time realistically and used systematic study procedures that he was able to cope successfully with his assignments.

The will to succeed. The third essential — the will to succeed in college — requires a certain clarity of purpose. In talking with literally hundreds of students, I have found that a major difference between success and failure is *a well-defined and realistic goal*. It is almost impossible to work constructively without one. A clear goal supplies motivation and the confidence that comes only from knowing where one is going. This healthy state of mind in turn channels energy into productive work, whereas uncertainty diffuses effort and tempts the mind to wander from the job. A goal gives purpose to academic life, and students who have a purpose find studying easier and grades higher.

Contrary to popular belief, the student with a goal is a good deal freer than the one with only a vague or feeble idea of direction. Having a purpose does not preclude a change of purpose. Actually, the student who is doing well is the only one who is free to change. For example, an engineering student who is getting good grades can easily transfer to a premedical or a liberal arts course; but one with poor grades cannot make the change, because the other school or department will not accept him.

DEFINING YOUR GOAL

Just what *is* a goal? Whenever I ask an unsuccessful student about his goal, he usually tells me he wants "to get a liberal education." Only after he tries, more or less fumblingly, to explain what a liberal education is, does he realize that he has been as vague in his thinking about his goal as in his thinking about his studies. It is praiseworthy to strive for a liberal education, but meaningless unless one knows what one means by a liberal education and hence has some idea of the concrete terms in which this aim is to be achieved. The student might ask himself what specific knowledge and abilities he associates with a liberally educated person. Let us suppose he comes up with the following: the ability to write and speak well, competence in a foreign language, a broad knowledge of literature, history, and economics, acquaintance with at least one of the natural sciences. To translate this concept into practice, he might then list all the courses he thinks essential to the kind of education he wants, in terms of the kind of person he wants to be, keeping in mind that a "liberal" education implies scope, breadth, freedom to acquire knowledge beyond the immediately practical and useful. He should also talk over his ideas about education with his adviser and other members of the faculty. Then, with a revised list of subjects and courses, he can plan his program in intelligent detail. He has set a standard which he can use, from time to time, as a measuring stick. Individual courses will then have a specific purpose in an over-all scheme, and the student, by thinking through to his goal, will have taken a long step toward academic success. He will have a *reason* to study.

A director of a large counseling service has said that students in academic trouble are usually those with no clearly defined goal. Such a goal is so necessary to success that one large university is planning to require each applicant to write out his academic goal, and to use this statement as one of the chief criteria for admission.

I urge you to write out your own academic goal in some detail. Only then will a "still small voice" within tell you whether you have defined it clearly. It is easy to rationalize vagueness and to protest that you are above so elementary an exercise. But a little reflection upon the value of a well-defined goal should convince you otherwise. After writing out your goal, place it where you can read it over now and then, to remind yourself that you have a job to do.

2

Scheduling Your Time

The way we use time — or waste it — is largely a matter of habit patterns. In this chapter we shall see how the efficient use of time is related to improved study habits and better academic work.

It is not easy to change old habits. They become deeply entrenched and we become proficient in them. But if they are bad habits, they put a ceiling on achievement. Let me cite an example. I learned to play tennis with an unorthodox grip and got to be pretty good in spite of it, though I realized I was always outplayed by opponents using an orthodox grip. I hated to give up what skill I had and go through an awkward period of re-learning. When I did change, my game was poor, as I had expected; but with practice it was soon better than before — eventually much better than it could ever have been with the old grip.

It takes determination to change, and the will to make painful adjustments. But the decision to change brings the chance for a better future. If you find that you need to adopt new study techniques, give them a fair trial. You are almost certain to improve much sooner than you would think.

THE VALUE OF A TIME SCHEDULE

One means to good study habits is scheduling your time. Many students rationalize that they want to be flexible and not tied down. They mean, usually, that they want to be flexible enough to have as many coffee breaks and bull sessions as opportunity offers. Such students seldom have time enough to finish their assignments.

To see where your time goes, and how well you use it, keep a diary of your daily activities (see Figure 2–1, page 6) for one typical week. You may find, to take just one example, that your average "ten-minute" coffee break is nearer forty minutes. At the end of the week, add up the time spent in each activity. Analyze this summary to see how you can avoid dribbling away minutes and so save hours for both recreation and study.

If you are one of those who "never have a minute to spare," you will be interested in the following:

A recent study[1] showed that in a typical week students at one university spent time as follows in four essential activities:

Study	19.8 hours
Class and laboratory	18.7
Sleep	49.3
Meals	10.7
Total	98.5 hours

Subtract this amount from 168 (the number of hours in a week) and you still have 69.5 hours unaccounted for — almost 10 hours a day. But in spite of this wealth of time, students are always running out of it. This paradox argues two things: inefficient study habits and poor scheduling. This book is devoted to the first of these problems, and this chapter to the second.

A time schedule will not make a robot of you. Rather, it will provide order and discipline, and so *free* you to do your best. A schedule is a plan to help you get things done in an orderly way. It also keeps you informed on your own progress and broadens your horizon by giving you time to do things you could not do without it. It saves time spent in indecision, and so prevents worry, hasty improvisation, and the feeling that you are always on the run.

ALLOTMENT OF TIME

The oft-repeated rule-of-thumb that you should study two hours for every hour in class is a rough guide at best. Most assignments are made in terms of pages or chapters, not hours. A professor seldom, if ever, says, "Study economics for two hours before our next meeting." He says, "Read Chapter 3," or "pages 200–240"; or, "Find out all you can about the topic discussed in class today." It is impossible to schedule day-to-day study in fixed numbers of hours, but it is helpful to keep two general points in mind:

1. Scheduling fixed hours is realistic only when reviewing or studying for a test. Even here, studying for a required amount of time is not an end in itself. One must understand what he has studied before he can say he has finished.

2. All of us know that the time required per subject varies from student to student and from subject to subject. One student writes English themes easily but grasps chemistry only with great effort; another breezes through mathematics but has a terrible struggle with history. Hygiene takes less time than French. To schedule realistically, a student must know what he can do with his various subjects in how much time. Within his schedule,

[1] Arthur A. Dole, "College Students Report on the Use of Time," *The Personnel and Guidance Journal*, Vol. 37, No. 9 (May, 1959), 635.

Time		Time Used	Activity-Description	
Start	End			
11:45	7:45	8:00	Sleep	
7:45	8:15	:30	Dress	
8:15	8:40	:25	Breakfast	
8:40	9:00	:20	Nothing	Look over textbook assignment and previous lecture notes.
9:00	10:00	1:00	Class-History	
10:00	10:40	:40	Break-Coffee	Break too long and too soon after breakfast.
10:40	11:00	:20	Nothing	Look over previous lecture notes.
11:00	12:00	1:00	Class-English	
12:00	12:35	:35	Lunch	
12:35	2:00	1:25	Reading-Magazine	Reserve recreational reading for after finishing assignments.
2:00	4:00	2:00	Lab-Chemistry	
4:00	5:30	1:30	Recreation-Volleyball	
5:30	6:00	:30	Nothing	Could read magazine now.
6:00	7:00	1:00	Dinner	
7:00	8:00	1:00	Nap	Not a good idea. Better finish work, then a good night's sleep.
8:00	8:50	:50	Study-Math	
8:50	9:20	:30	Break	Too long.
9:20	10:00	:40	Study-Math	
10:00	10:50	:50	Bull Session	Good, if basic work is done.
10:50	11:30	:40	Study-Psychology	Insufficient time allotted.
11:30	11:45	:15	Ready for bed	

Suggestions for making better use of time.

FIGURE 2–1

Record of One Day's Activities

he must allocate his time accordingly. Experience, and the desire to do more work in less time, should lead, after some trial and error, to fairly accurate planning.

MASSED AND DISTRIBUTED STUDY

Ideally, when studying a new assignment, one should study until he masters it. As much massed study as is possible preserves continuity of context and effort.

When reviewing, however, it is better to distribute rather than mass the time devoted to any one subject. For example, in allotting six hours to review for a French test, you will learn more in six one-hour periods spaced through the week than in one six-hour period. Psychological studies show that in the intervals between the six one-hour periods, incidental learning continues. The sum of learning gained in six distributed hours is thus greater than that in six massed hours. In addition, you will be less susceptible to boredom. But it is not always easy to schedule six well-spaced hours in one week, and a compromise of three two-hour periods may be the best you can do. Remember, though, that at the end of six distributed hours of study you still have not necessarily mastered the subject or finished the job.

DAYTIME STUDY PERIODS

One cause of poor work in college is failure to make use of short periods of time. I am dismayed every time I hear a student call an hour between classes a "dead" hour. For those who feel this way the hour is dead indeed. Yet some of the most important lessons of our lives are learned in less time.

Many students can do more during the day, when they are fresh, than in comparable periods of time in the evening. One engineering student, who was consistently on the honor list, told me that he attended good movies or read for pleasure after nine o'clock every night. His secret was to make every minute count. Concentrated effort during the day gave him free time in the evenings. Whether he knew it or not, he was practicing a sound psychological principle: he was rewarding himself for work well done.

Free periods before recitation classes and after lecture classes provide particularly valuable opportunities for study. For a course in which you recite and discuss, it is an advantage to study just before class, so that the material will be fresh in your mind and your thinking stimulated. For a lecture course, retention and understanding are aided by a review of your lecture notes immediately after class — or at your first possible opportunity. Many of my former students who formed the habit of reviewing notes directly after a lecture found it so successful that they continually urge me to stress its value. They make the following points: first, immediate review gives more thorough understanding and provides a basis for a better grasp of succeeding lectures and reading assignments; second, it saves time to review the lecture before forgetting sets in, and it eases the task of reviewing for examinations; finally, grades improve in proportion to the time and effort put into immediate review.

TAKING BREAKS

Most students report that they need to take ten-minute breaks during an extended study period. I advise them to take a ten-minute break whenever they feel the need for one; this minimizes "clock watching." More important than the length of a break is what you do when you take one. Stand up, walk around, or just stare out the window if you like — but keep in mind the subject you are studying: speculate about it, argue with yourself about some problem just encountered in your reading, take the opposite view and wonder why it would not hold up. By thinking positively about the subject, you not only maintain continuity of study but improve your grasp. Most students who do this find that they usually take less than a ten-minute break, since they are eager to get on with the subject, and that they do not need a warm-up period when they resume studying. Without this technique it is all too easy to abuse the break by making it too long.

SCHEDULING RECREATION

In planning your time, be sure to have a reasonable balance between work and recreation. It is unrealistic to omit from a time-plan the physical and social activities necessary to a well-balanced life. If your schedule is realistic, you will be encouraged to follow it. If it is not, you will be tempted to give up the whole idea of scheduling.

Developing good study habits through scheduling your time does not mean becoming a greasy grind. The student who makes himself a slave to study may become an unattractive personality and may study less efficiently than he thinks he does. On the other hand, an imbalance that permits extracurricular activities to outweigh studies probably accounts for more failures in college than anything else. Here are a few suggestions to help you avoid this pitfall:

1. It is natural to want social activity. It is natural to have dates, take part in sports, go to the movies, join fraternities and sororities and clubs. But remember that these are adjuncts to learning, and that learning is the real reason for going to college.

2. Students who try to do too many things are likely to spend too much time away from study. Few people can play on an athletic team, belong to a fraternity, work part-time in the dining hall, and do acceptable academic work — all at once. Something has to give, and it will probably be study.

3. The plea that you have an assignment to complete, a paper to write, or a problem to review is universally accepted in college. Contrary to some opinion, the Big Man on Campus is not the man who fails his courses. Such a man is not very big, and he is usually not on campus very long.

HOW TO MAKE A TIME SCHEDULE

The specimen weekly time-plan shown in Figure 2–2 illustrates some *general principles* of scheduling. The outlined boxes represent class periods, and the allotment of time for study, recreation, and the requirements of daily living revolves around these fixed class hours as discussed in the analysis on page 11.

But for practical use, week after week, a schedule such as this would be too rigid and detailed to serve as a realistic guide. Some weeks you will have special assignments that will take more time than is provided by so general a plan. And, just because your schedule says you must study history at that hour, wouldn't you be foolish to miss hearing the speech of a world-famous statesman who is visiting your campus?

Clearly, there would have to be weekly revisions and variations. But to draw up so detailed a schedule every week would take a good deal of time — time better spent in studying. And yet, in the long run, it would be even more wasteful of time to make no schedule at all.

Seeking a happy medium, we offer a system which is not an iron framework yet gives support in using time effectively and realistically. There is no need to schedule in detail, week after week, the many activities that are fixed throughout the term: meals, sleep, class hours, free time on Saturdays and Sundays, and the like. These constitute the master pattern of your week and should soon become established as matters of habit. The practice of using between-class hours to brush up in advance for recitation and discussion courses and to review notes taken in lecture courses should also become so habitual that there is no need to schedule every such free hour in detail. Here, then, is a plan for a schedule that is easy to make, practical, and genuinely helpful:

First (Figure 2–3), make out a master schedule for the term and fill in your fixed activities: rising and retiring times, meals, classes, and weekend time to be held in reserve for non-study activities. You may also, if you wish, include fixed times for recreational reading or for reviewing notes. The empty boxes now represent hours which you can schedule for study.

Second (Figure 2–4), make a weekly schedule sheet which revolves around your assignments. The format is simple: draw a horizontal line to divide a lined sheet of paper in half. Use the upper half to list your subjects, assignments, estimated study times, and due dates. Then, using the due dates and the estimated times as control factors, check your master schedule for hours available. Choose enough available hours to do each job, and write them on the appropriate line on the bottom half of the weekly schedule sheet. *Then stick to your schedule.* Give study hours top priority. As long as you do, the remaining free hours will be really free.

Students find that this way of scheduling really works: no countless boxes to fill in; no intricate maze to grope through; best of all, no more guilty conscience from schedules laboriously made and quietly abandoned.

9

Time	Mon.	Tues.	Wed.	Thurs.	Fri.	Sat.	Sun.
7-8	← Dress & Breakfast →						↑
8-9	History	Study Chem.	History	Study Chem.	History	Study Chem.	
9-10	Study History	Phy.Ed.	Study History	Phy.Ed.	Study History	Phy.Ed.	Church, Recreation, Conversation, Recreational Reading
10-11	Study French	Chem.	Study French	Chem.	Study French	Chem.	
11-12	French	Study Chem.	French	Study Chem.	French	Study Chem.	
12-1	← Lunch →					↑	
1-2	Math.	ROTC	Math	ROTC	Math		
2-3	Study Math	Library: Theme	Study Math	↑	Study Math	Recreation, Conversation, Special Proj., Reading, Extra Work on Difficult Subjects, Thorough Review.	
3-4	Study English	"	Study English	Chem. Lab.	Study English		
4-5	English	"	English	↓	English		
5-6	← Recreation →						
6-7	← Dinner →						↓
7-8	Study English	Study Math	Study English	Study Math	Study English		English Theme
8-9	Study French	Study History	Study French	Study History	Study French		English Theme
9-10	Review English	Review French	Review History	Review Math	Review Chem.		Study History
10-11	← Recreational Reading →						
11-12	← Conversation, Sleep →					↓	

FIGURE 2-2

Some Principles of Scheduling

Assume that this schedule is your own, and study it in the light of the analysis on the opposite page.

Monday through Friday/Saturday

7–8 A.M.   Preclude the frantic dash and the gobbled (or skipped) breakfast by getting up on time.

12–1 P.M.   Take a full, leisurely hour for lunch.

5–6   Relax before dinner — your reward for a day of conscientious work.

7–9   Keep up with current notes and assignments by systematic studying.

9–10   To forestall cramming at quiz and examination times, give some time every day to a review of previous assignments and ground covered to date.

10   A "cease-study" time of ten o'clock is an incentive to work hard during the day and early evening.

10–12   You should devote some time every day to reading books that truly interest you. Recreational reading and conversation help you "unwind" for a good night's sleep.

Monday-Wednesday-Friday

9–10 A.M.   Use the free period after history (a lecture course) to study your lecture notes.

10–11   Since French (at 11) is a recitation course, prepare by studying during the free period that precedes class.

2–3 P.M.   In math class (1–2) problems are usually discussed and worked out on the blackboard. It is wise to take notes on both discussion and blackboard work. Then, because math problems can quickly become "cold," use this free period to go over the work covered in class during the preceding hour.

3–4   English (4–5) is often a discussion period. Use the free hour to study and warm up in advance.

7–8   Your evening study time begins. Start with English, your last class, so that any notes you took can be reviewed before forgetting takes place.

8–9   Study French, giving priority to the notes and assignments of the day.

Tuesday-Thursday-Saturday

8–9 A.M.   Since chemistry (10–11) is your "hard" subject, you build your morning study program around it. An hour's study before class will make the class period more meaningful.

11–12   Another hour's study immediately after chemistry class will help you to remember the work covered in class and to move more readily to the next assignment.

Special

Tuesday 2–5, library: theme ⎫
Sunday, 7–9, English theme ⎭   For some assignments you will need to schedule blocs of time in order to do research or to develop and follow up ideas.

Saturday from noon on is left unscheduled — for recreation — for special projects to which you must devote a concentrated period of time — for extra work on difficult subjects — for thorough review.

Sunday is your day until evening. Study history before you go to bed, because it is the first class you'll have, on Monday morning.

	MON.	TUES.	WED.	THUR.	FRI.	SAT.	SUN.
7-8	←————————— Dress + Breakfast —————————→						Recreation + Church
8-9	History		History		History		
9-10		English		English		English	
10-11		Chem.		Chem.		Chem. Lab. ↓	
11-12	French		French		French		
12-1	←————————————— Lunch —————————————→						
1-2	Math	ROTC	Math	ROTC	Math	↑	
2-3	Phys. Ed.		Phys. Ed.		Phys. Ed.		
3-4						Review	
4-5							
5-6						↓	
6-7	←————————————— Dinner —————————————→						↓
7-8						↑	
8-9						Recreation	
9-10							
10-11							
11-12	←————————————— Sleep —————————————→					↓	

SPECIAL NOTES

Monday	
Tuesday	
Wednesday	
Thursday	
Friday	
Saturday	
Sunday	

FIGURE 2–3

A Master Schedule

Subject	Assignment	Estimated Time	Due date	Time
History	150 pages	6½ hrs.	Wed.	8:00
English	Paper	12 hrs.	Sat.	9:00
Chemistry	20 pages-Read	4 hrs.	Thurs.	10:00
Math	20 problems	6 hrs.	Fri.	1:00
French	Lesson 5	4 hrs.	Wed.	11:00

Day	Tasks			
Mon.	Read History: Start French:	9:30–10:30	3:30–6:00	7:00–10:00 10:00–11:00
Tues.	Read Chemistry: Finish French:		2:00–6:00	7:00–10:00
Wed.	Do Math : Start English: — Paper —	9:30–10:30	3:30–5:30	7:00–11:00
Thurs.	Finish Math : English Paper : — Write —	2:00–5:00		7:00–11:00
Fri.	English Paper : 9:30–10:30 — Revise & Polish —			7:00–10:00
Sat.				
Sun.				

FIGURE 2–4

A Weekly Schedule

3

A Sense of Order

The human mind seeks order in everything, and feels satisfied only when it can fit a new experience into the pattern of beliefs and experiences it has already built for itself. Order is essential in all of living, and it is certainly essential in learning. To grasp and retain the masses of material you will be required to master in college, you must learn to understand the pattern — the order or organization — of what you read in books and hear in lectures. Only then will your learning be meaningful and stick with you. Only then will you be able to organize your own themes, essays, and examination papers in a way that will show others that you have effectively learned and understood.

The organization of every book, article, essay, speech, or lecture is as much a part of its author's thinking as the facts and ideas he has to convey. Even a poem or a piece of imaginative prose does not "just happen" through sheer genius or inspiration, but requires careful and conscious planning; and a study of its structure can further one's understanding of the work — though since a poem, for example, is much more than its content, this kind of approach is less rewarding for creative than for expository materials. In any case, the organization of any piece of writing is a highly individual matter, and no pattern is ever exactly repeated. But certain elements of organization can be identified as common to all coherent presentations. If you develop sensitivity to these — in your reading and listening and in your own writing — you should always know where you have been, where you are at the moment, and where you are going.

FIVE ELEMENTS OF ORGANIZATION

You know that every effective piece of writing has a beginning, a middle, and an end. In addition, it has a direction or goal, and it has numerous signposts to guide you along the way. This may sound ridiculously simple, yet it is the heart of the problem both of grasping the facts and ideas presented by others and of organizing and presenting your own. Let's examine in detail the elements of good organization. Though we shall speak mainly in terms of written presentations, the same principles apply to oral ones such as lectures and speeches.

1. *The introduction* to any discussion is usually brief in relation to the whole. In one way or another, it announces the subject and gives you some clue to its importance and to the way the author plans to treat it. The introduction may define terms, give historical background, or summarize prerequisite knowledge. It is the beginning of the journey, the springboard, the launching pad.

2. *The thesis* states the purpose or scope of the discussion, together with the exact problem to be considered. It may also foreshadow the conclusion to be reached. The thesis may occupy a sentence or a paragraph, rarely more. But it is crucial, and if you miss it you may flounder aimlessly to the end. When you find the thesis, mark it or make a note of it, and keep it firmly in mind as you read on.

3. *The body* of the discussion usually bulks nine-tenths of the whole. This is the point-by-point presentation of data or of steps in an argument by which the author attempts to amplify his thesis, support or prove his point of view, or give his information. Once you have the thesis clearly in mind, your main job in reading is to see *how* the author develops or supports it. This means relating his topics, as he takes them up, to his thesis and to each other, so that you can group facts and dates, processes and techniques, causes and effects, in a meaningful order and hence more readily remember them.

4. *Transitions,* or guideposts, are invaluable clues to organization. Transitional words or phrases such as *formerly* and *meanwhile* help to establish the time frame; *on the contrary* and *in another sense* signal a change in point of view; *still worse* and *indeed* add emphasis. Other transitional words and phrases express precise relationships of many kinds, and it is as important to know these as it is for a mathematician to know the meaning of plus and minus. Here are some of them: *also, besides, consequently, furthermore, however, hence, in addition, likewise, moreover, nevertheless, so, still, therefore, thus, then.* These words and many others point the direction which the reader should take in following the development of ideas and concepts.

Most good lecturers also are careful about transitions, and use more obvious ones than writers generally use. Note the contrast in the examples shown in Figure 3–1.

5. *The conclusion* pulls together main ideas presented in the introduction and developed in the body of the discussion. Even in the conclusion a transitional phrase such as *for these reasons* or *as we have seen* often provides the signal that you are about to read a summary or a conclusion.

You will be amazed how much easier it is to follow a reading assignment or a lecture once you have in mind the general principle of organization and gain skill in following organization as you read or listen. With practice, too, you will learn to see when a writer or speaker is successful or unsuccessful

	WRITER	SPEAKER
BEGINNING	Nothing in English history contains such tragic overtones as the Battle of Hastings.	Last hour we discussed the political events that led to the Battle of Hastings. Let us turn now to the tragedy itself.
THESIS	But a divided England was less the cause of downfall than Norman lances vs. English axes.	Thus the English had to fight without the army that was still in the north. More important, the Normans wore armor and fought on horseback, while the English had no armor and fought on foot.
TRANSITION	The Normans fought with propaganda too; the Pope was on their side.	Third, it is important to .remember that the Pope favored William, and his standard on the field frightened many English from the battle.
CONCLUSION	Everything lent William power and conspired to change the fate of England.	To sum up, then, a divided England, superior weapons, and the favor of the Church gave William the advantage in every area of the conflict.

FIGURE 3–1

Transitions as Clues to Organization

*A lecturer uses more obvious transitions than a writer
to help his audience move from point to point.*

in organizing his materials effectively, and you will be able to evaluate the validity of his conclusion from the way he has presented his information or supported his thesis. You will also, through learning to follow organizational pattern, learn how to relate what you read and hear to a meaningful pattern of your own.

KINDS OF ORGANIZATION

Beyond these general elements of coherent organization, there are certain kinds of organizational arrangements which are largely shaped by the nature of the material itself. Biography, history, and narrative, for example, fall readily into a *chronological* pattern. Description, as of a house, machine, or geographical area, is likely to assume a *spatial* pattern. But most expository presentations — and this includes the greater part of what you will read for your assignments and will hear in lectures — are *topical*, that is, arranged according to logical divisions of the thought, rather than by order of occurrence in time or space.

Chronological and Spatial Arrangement. Once you detect chronological or spatial arrangement, the pattern is generally not hard to follow. Most stories, biographies, and historical accounts proceed steadily from past to present, though occasionally a narrative will begin in the middle or even at the end and then go back to the beginning. When this happens there are usually clues, but the reader who has never encountered this kind of arrangement may be confused the first few times he meets it. On the other hand, nearly everyone is familiar with the so-called "flashback" technique, in which the main line of the story is occasionally interrupted by scenes which describe earlier events. Straight chronological order is also used in expository writing which explains a process — for example, how to pitch a tent, make a pair of shoes, or write a term paper. In such writing, the problem is less to find the pattern than to master the steps in the procedure.

Spatial arrangement usually offers even fewer complications. A geography of the United States may move from New England to the Middle Atlantic States to the Southeast, and so on; it will almost never skip from Maine to California and back to Massachusetts. But within such a large spatial pattern, there may be a number of topical headings which are not always immediately apparent.

Topical Arrangement. "Topical arrangement" is a broad term which may cover a variety of patterns. Thus under each of the spatial divisions suggested for the geography mentioned above, there may be discussed such subjects as agriculture, industry, climate, topography, and population. If these are taken up in one-two-three order, without indication of any particular relationships among them, we have the simplest of all topical schemes, one which sets up topical headings or categories merely for the sake of presenting one thing at a time in clear and orderly fashion. A more complex kind of topical arrangement — and one far more common — makes use of relationships among topics, particularly *cause and effect.* Thus a geographer may have the thesis that climate and topography influence agriculture, and that these in turn influence population. He may therefore begin his discussion of New England by describing the thin and rocky soil, the hills and mountains, and then point out that for these reasons this is a poor agricultural region. He may then describe New England's seaports, fisheries, and abundance of water power, and show how these and other factors have affected commercial and industrial development. In both parts of the discussion he is using a topical arrangement which leads from cause to effect — and these relationships become as much a part of his total meaning as the facts of climate, rainfall, and production.

Many topical arrangements are even more complex. An economist discussing the great crash of 1929 would almost certainly divide his subject into three main parts: events leading up to the crash (causes); the catas-

How to bring together lover & bird

Locale: Close space
↓
like a frame

Familiar chamber Rich in articles
↓
leading to Beauty

How to get bird in —
↓
Window
↓
Tapping like knocking door

Contrast: Fierce night out Quiet inside

Contrast: Pallas — white Bird — black

unusual, and some altogether novel effects, arising from an extension of the application of the principles of rhyme and alliteration.

The next point to be considered was the mode of bringing together the lover and the Raven—and the first branch of this consideration was the *locale*. For this the most natural suggestion might seem to be a forest, or the fields—but it has always appeared to me that a close *circumscription of space* is absolutely necessary to the effect of insulated incident:—it has the force of a frame to a picture. It has an indisputable moral power in keeping concentrated the attention, and, of course, must not be confounded with mere unity of place.

I determined, then, to place the lover in his chamber—in a chamber rendered sacred to him by memories of her who had frequented it. The room is represented as richly furnished—this in mere pursuance of the ideas I have already explained on the subject of Beauty, as the sole true poetical thesis.

The *locale* being thus determined, I had now to introduce the bird—and the thought of introducing him through the window, was inevitable. The idea of making the lover suppose, in the first instance, that the flapping of the wings of the bird against the shutter, is a "tapping" at the door, originated in a wish to increase, by prolonging, the reader's curiosity, and in a desire to admit the incidental effect arising from the lover's throwing open the door, finding all dark, and thence adopting the half-fancy that it was the spirit of his mistress that knocked.

I made the night tempestuous, first, to account for the Raven's seeking admission, and secondly, for the effect of contrast with the (physical) serenity within the chamber.

I made the bird alight on the bust of Pallas, also for the effect of contrast between the marble and the plumage—it being understood that the bust was absolutely *suggested* by the bird—the bust of *Pallas* being chosen, first, as most in keeping with the scholarship of the lover, and, secondly, for the sonorousness of the word, Pallas, itself.

About the middle of the poem, also, I have availed myself of the force of contrast, with a view of deepening the ultimate impression. For example, an air of the fantastic—approaching as nearly to the ludicrous as was admissible—is given to the Raven's

FIGURE 3–2

Organization in the Creative Process

In his essay "The Philosophy of Composition," Edgar Allan Poe analyzes the careful and conscious planning of his poem "The Raven."

trophe itself; and its aftermath (results). But he would not necessarily have to discuss them in this order. For dramatic effect he might begin with a description of those black days in October 1929 when ruined investors were throwing themselves from the windows of Wall Street office buildings, and move from that to a description of the plummeting stock market which caused their despair and suicide. Following the event itself, he might then go back to enumerate and analyze the causes of the crash — inflated stock values, excessive installment buying, and so on. Finally, he might discuss the long, slow recovery during the years of the great depression in the 1930's, the far-reaching results of the central event.

In following any topical organization, it is necessary to be alert to relationships, particularly causes and results. The clues to these are often suggested in the introductory paragraphs or chapters of books and articles, and in the first minutes of lectures — so frequently lost in the flurry of opening one's notebook and finding the place. Further clues are contained in transitions. Any extended discourse is a complex of facts and relationships. In many of the books you read, the task will be made simpler by centered headings, side headings, and summaries, constant reminders of where you are in the discussion and how a topic relates to what has gone before.

A student who understands the basic types of organization can do a better job when he writes themes, research papers, and answers to examination questions than one who does not. The use of an appropriate pattern not only helps him put his thoughts in an order which is understandable to the reader, but enables him to say more nearly what he wants to say.

The mind works best when it works logically, and mental energy is best used when thinking follows a logical plan. Orderly thinking can become habitual; and when it does, the student is not only more productive, but he achieves confidence and the mental balance which reflects a mature personality.

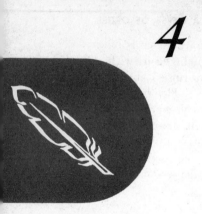

4

In the Classroom:

Listening and Taking Notes

Most students come in contact with the lecture system for the first time after they enter college. And most students, because it is new to them, soak up a good deal of nonsense about what to do and what not to do in a lecture. Let's get this nonsense out of the way first; you will then be ready to learn how to get the most out of a lecture. The heart of the matter is learning to listen actively and to take good notes at the same time.

SOME NONSENSE ABOUT LECTURES

You will be sure to hear that you can get more out of a lecture if you don't take notes. This could be true if you took an examination right after the lecture. But you don't; you take one weeks or months later, and you can forget a lot by then. You can't review the lecture without good notes.

You may hear that you should take notes only on the main points of a lecture. This just doesn't work. Noting a point after you have decided that it is important interferes with your listening to the next point. On the other hand, don't think you must record every word the lecturer says; rather, be alert to take down the facts and ideas which form the step-by-step development of the topic.

You may hear that you should reflect upon the lecturer's ideas as they are being presented. This is highly impractical. When you emerge from your reflections on point one, you are apt to hear the lecturer say, "and point number four is. . . ." This does not mean that you should take notes unthinkingly, like a tape recorder. But extended reflection should come later, assisted by complete notes taken during the lecture.

You may hear that you should convert the lecturer's words into your own. This also is seldom possible in a fast-moving lecture. Formulating concepts in your own words should come later, in your study time.

You may hear that you should take notes in formal outline — I, A, 1, a, etc. The outline form does have some advantages in organizing the material, but it has disadvantages too. By the time you decide whether a point is major or minor the lecturer may be paragraphs ahead of you. Also, until you have the complete pattern of the lecture, you cannot always be sure that you are making accurate decisions on the coordination and subordination of topics, subtopics, and supporting materials.

Students who take few notes, or none at all, are seldom short on excuses. They complain that the instructor is a poor lecturer, that his material is poorly organized and hard to follow, that he isn't saying anything important enough to take notes on, or that he is only repeating what is in the textbook. Or they argue that note-taking distracts them from listening. Yet these are the very students who consistently find themselves at the bottom of the class. They fail for two reasons. Since they do not feel that anything important is being said, they do not listen attentively. And since they do not take notes, they do not have the lecturer's ideas and information as a basis for further study. A good lecture either expands material in the text by giving more details and fuller explanations, or it supplements the text by covering different material or taking a different point of view.

THE FIRST STEP: GOOD LISTENING

To get the most out of a lecture, you must listen actively. Good listening requires alertness, and the key to remaining alert in class is preparation. A good rule is to review the last reading assignment, and your notes on the preceding lecture, before going to class. Also, spend a few minutes speculating on what points today's lecture may cover.

1. In class, assume a position of physical alertness. A slouch is not conducive to good note-taking. Also, many students pay closer attention if they sit near the lecturer; this is especially important for those with visual or hearing difficulties.

2. Be mentally alert. Concentrate on the lecturer; don't follow the crack in the ceiling with your eyes or count stitches while knitting — in fact, don't knit. Become so involved with the lecture that you are aware of virtually nothing else.

3. Maintain a proper mental attitude. Try to learn all you can; even "dull" subjects become interesting once you are involved. It helps to realize that the lecturer is saving you hours of hard work by organizing the salient points of the course for you. The more you learn in class, the easier it will be to complete your assignment and the better you will understand it.

4. Do not be distracted by the speaker's mannerisms, his method of delivery, or the quality of his voice. Concentrate on what he says, not on oddities of delivery or platform behavior. Dr. Ralph W. Gerard, Professor of Neurophysiology in the Mental Health Research Institute at the University of Michigan, tells a memorable story on this point:

> I remember a college course in chemistry in which the lecturer spoke in a monotone and would have earned a low grade in elocution; he was, nonetheless, a superb teacher and gave a clear, logical, organized presenta-

tion of the guiding ideas. In a particular lecture he told how the great German chemist, Emil Fischer, had proved the molecular structure of a group of sugars and so put modern organic chemistry on its feet. At the end of the hour two of us walked blindly from the room as from a magnificent concert, smack into some obstruction in the hall. We simply didn't see it. One can, indeed, become as immersed in an aesthetic experience based on the beauty of intellectual processes as in one based on the beauty of sensory experiences.

5. Listen with your mind, not your emotions. If the speaker uses a word you don't like, or makes a point contrary to your beliefs, don't stop listening — you'll only be defeating yourself. Rehearsing devastating rebuttals to hurl at him prevents you from hearing additional, perhaps qualifying, comments. Jot down questions and specific points of disagreement so you won't forget them; then go on listening. If they still seem significant after the lecture, raise them during the discussion period. Listening with your mind, or registering what you hear, does not mean that you must *accept* everything you hear. To find yourself occasionally in opposition is a good thing, since it means that you are thinking about what you hear and relating it to what you already know.

6. When it is appropriate to do so, raise questions in class. Some lecturers follow a tight schedule which leaves no time for questions; others do not. You can soon tell. When time allows, most instructors welcome sincere questions, though they are quick to recognize those that are ill-considered or intended to impress. A good question helps you relate new knowledge to other ideas and fix it in your mind. Don't be afraid of being laughed at. Even if you ask a question that has already been answered, or one which is obvious or even silly, the worst that can happen to you is a sharp reply and a moment's embarrassment.

To ask useful questions, note points not clear to you as you read your assignments. Discuss these with your classmates, and if the answers still don't come clear, raise questions in class. Be sure to follow the class discussion closely so that your questions will be pertinent. Finally, stop speaking when you have made your point; time is at a premium.

In some courses, large lecture meetings are supplemented by smaller discussion groups. These allow you to ask questions on both lectures and reading. Don't miss this chance.

THE SECOND STEP: ORDERLINESS

Before we discuss techniques of note-taking which have proved successful, here are twenty general suggestions which will help you take better notes. Added up, these mean: *be alert, be orderly, be systematic; and don't let things slide.*

1. Attend lectures faithfully. The lecture system is the backbone of many courses, and a complete set of notes is usually crucial.

2. Keep notes for each course in one place, in a separate notebook or section of a notebook.

3. Take notes on one side of the page only. Often it is a great help to spread out the pages and *see* the pattern of a lecture.

4. Use a loose-leaf notebook or a file folder for your notes rather than a notebook with a fixed binding.

5. Record the name and number of the course, the date, and the lecturer's name on the first sheet for each lecture. This is a safeguard against loss or mix-up of notes.

6. Use large sheets of paper to give yourself room to indent and to see the pattern of your notes. The standard size for a large notebook is $8\frac{1}{2} \times 11$ inches.

7. Do not doodle or knit. Any manual activity of this kind inhibits note-taking, interferes with concentration, and breaks eye-contact with the lecturer, whose gestures and facial expressions give important clues for understanding and remembering.

8. Make your notes complete and clear enough so that they will have meaning for you weeks and months later. You need not write in full sentences, however, since note-taking is a process of selection, condensation, and compression.

9. Write legibly. Later when you review, legible handwriting will let you concentrate on ideas and facts rather than on deciphering your notes. It also saves the time it would otherwise take to put scrawled notes into typewritten form. Copying notes is not a form of review but merely a mechanical process, wasteful of time.

10. Leave blanks for words, phrases, or ideas you think you may have missed. Directly after the lecture, ask the instructor or a fellow student to help you fill the gaps.

11. Develop your own system of enumeration and indention. Don't indent so far that you are crowded into a small area at the right-hand side of the page.

12. Develop abbreviations of common words and recurring terms. This will give you more time both to listen and to write.

13. Use a symbol (such as an asterisk, arrow, or underline) to mark ideas the lecturer emphasizes.

14. Mark off assignments that are mixed in with the lecture. Similarly, note and mark off any books or other references the lecturer mentions; these will be valuable guides to further reading.

15. Separate your own thoughts from the lecturer's. It is an excellent practice to jot down questions, your own examples, ideas, and references; but make sure you bracket or otherwise label these as yours, not his.

16. Be alert for clues. Often an instructor will say, "You'll see this later," or "This is important," or "This is a common pitfall." Following such clues, note important statements and put an asterisk or other symbol in the margin. Watch for enumerations — e.g., "The four steps in the process are as

follows." Watch for words such as "finally," "therefore," "furthermore," which may warn that an important point is about to be presented. Listen for other transitional words, phrases, or sentences which may signal the end of one main idea and the beginning of another.

17. Always record the lecturer's examples. They often clarify abstract ideas. Indicate the fact that they are examples; e.g., *Ex.*

18. Pay as close attention to the end of a lecture as to the beginning. Lecturers do not always pace themselves accurately, and may cram half the content into the last five or ten minutes. Record such packed finales as rapidly as you can, and if necessary, stay in your seat for a few extra minutes to write down as much as you can remember.

19. Record additional ideas of your own immediately after the lecture.

20. Review your notes after the lecture, and improve the organization if necessary.

Like any techniques, listening and note-taking improve with practice. If you really try, you will soon be able to keep up with the fastest lecturer.

The rest of this chapter describes several note-taking schemes which have proved helpful to many students. Study them and adopt the one that seems best to you. Perhaps you will want to try them all before you make a choice.

THE 2–5–1 FORMAT

Many students like the "2–5–1" format for lecture notes. Rule your notebook in three vertical columns as shown below (Figure 4–1), and you are ready to begin.

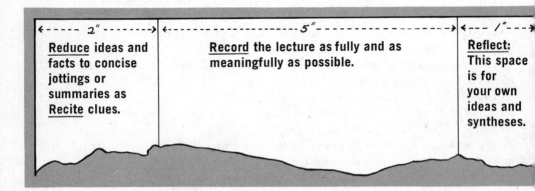

FIGURE 4–1

The 2–5–1 Format

This format provides the perfect opportunity for following through with the 5 R's of note-taking. Here they are:

1. *Record.* During the lecture, record in the 5-inch column as many meaningful facts and ideas as you can.

2. *Reduce.* As soon after as possible, summarize these ideas and facts concisely in the 2-inch column. Summarizing clarifies meanings and relationships, reinforces continuity, and strengthens memory. Also it is a way of preparing for examinations gradually and well ahead of time.

3. *Recite.* Now cover the 5-inch column. Using only your jottings in the 2-inch column as clues or "flags" to help you recall, say over the facts and ideas of the lecture as fully as you can, not by rote, but in your own words and with as much appreciation of the meaning as you can. Then, uncovering the notes, verify what you have said. This procedure is the most powerful study technique known to psychologists.

4. *Reflect.* Professor Hans Bethe, prominent nuclear physicist at Cornell University, has said that a student who goes only as far as his textbooks and lectures take him can become proficient but never creative. Creativity, even real mastery of a subject, comes only with reflection. Seeing new material in the light of what you already know is the only road to original ideas, for having an idea is nothing more than discovering a relationship not seen before. And it is impossible to have ideas without reflecting — i.e., thinking.

5. *Review.* If you will repeat Step 3 every week or so, you will retain most of what you have learned, and you will be able to use your knowledge to greater and greater effect.

Example 1. Figure 4–2 shows a page of good notes in the 2–5–1 format. The lecture notes, in the 5-inch column, are largely in topical outline form, though the individual items are detailed enough to be meaningful. One advantage of the outline form is that it shows relationships.[1]

The concise notations in the 2-inch column both summarize main points and provide clues for recitation.

In this case the 1-inch column (which may be used at any time) was filled in just before the mid-term examinations — and provided an excellent review. An advantage of making a synthesis or summary at examination time is that you can then look back at earlier lectures in the light of newer knowledge.

Example 2. Another page of good notes in the 2–5–1 format is shown in Figure 4–3. Here, too, the notes in the 5-inch column are in outline, but are closer to the sentence form than to the topical. Diagrams and examples are helpful aids in review. Notice that the assignment is written directly into the notes.

Here the notes in the 2-inch column are simple clues for recitation, not summaries. Notice, however, the listing of key terms at the top of the

[1] But remember the warning on pages 20–21.

October 10, 1956 — Soc. 102 — Prof. Oxford

A. Animism

Stick has mind-power.

   1. Object has supernatural power.

Power — mana

   2. Belief object has mind — a power.
   3. Animism associated with Polynesia.
   4. Power called *mana*. (not limited to objects)
     a. Objects accumulate mana.
       Ex. Good canoe has more mana than poor one.

Can gain or lose mana

     b. Objects can lose mana.
     c. People collect objects with lots of mana.
     d. Good person's objects collect mana.
     e. People, animals, plants have mana, too.
       Ex. Expert canoe builder has mana — imparts mana to canoe.

Good people have lots of mana

     f. Chief has lots of mana — too dangerous to get too close to chief — mana around head.

Too much mana = Tabu.

   5. Tabu
     a. Objects with powerful mana are tabu.

Use Tabu to regulate economy

     b. Chief can manipulate mana — If certain animal becoming scarce, can place tabu on animal for a while.

B. Magic

Cause & Effect (mixture) (rain)

   1. Science of primitive man — cause & effect.
   2. Make mixture (cause); Then it rains (effect).
     a. Don't know why it works, but when mixture made, rain comes.

Sympathetic = clay model

   3. Two kinds magic.
     a. Sympathetic — make model or form of person from clay, etc., then stick pins into object to hurt symbolized person.

Contagious = fingernail clippings

     b. Contagious magic
      (1) Need to possess an article belonging to another person.
      (2) Ex. Fingernail clippings. By doing harm to these objects, feel that harm can be thus transmitted.

Good or evil uses.

     c. All magic not necessarily evil — can be used for both good and evil.

Animism — power (mana) in objects, animals, or persons. Primitive way of explaining happenings to impose meaning upon the irrational.

Magic — (cause & effect) Method by which man feels that he had some measure of control over his environment — to solve his daily problems.

FIGURE 4-2

Lecture Notes in 2-5-1 Format

Outline form — mainly topical.

Key Terms:
apocalypse
millennium
regenerate
cataclysmic

Def. of
Apocalypse

Origin of idea
of apocalypse

Idea of
apocalypse in
theories of
history:

2 Greek ideas:
1. ——
2. ——

Hebrew view —

2 peculiarities
of Hebrew view:

(Biblio.)

Modern idea —
man taking
over.

Romantic Masterworks — Abrams 9/29/59
Topic: Background for Reading Apocalyptic Literature

Assignment:
Read Genesis and Revelations before next class meeting.

I. Def. of apocalypse: a vision of a new world —
the last days in which world is regenerate and (in New
Testament) all time stops and we're back in infinity.

II. Idea of apocalypse a Hebrew invention. Greeks
had nothing like it.

III. Various views of hist. & how apocalyptic idea
figures in them.

   A. First Greek view: the "cycle pattern" —
   "everything repeats itself:" "there's nothing
   new under the sun." Goes on w/o end:

   good times.
   bad times.

   B. 2nd Greek view: the "primitivists" — the best
   days were in the beginning & things going from
   bad to worse ever since.

                    Beginning.
   C. Hebrew view:
   1. History has beginning & an end — this peculiar
   to them: In the beginning, a heaven & earth —
   in the end, a new heaven & earth:
   2. Diagram of Hebrew view:

   Garden of Eden   1000 years of   then,
                      restored earth   end of
                                        earth
       Fall of man
            Christ
   but restoration delayed until "second coming".
   After the end, time stops and those deserving
   return to eternity — either to heaven or hell.

   3. Two peculiarities
      a. beginning and end — finite.
      b. right angle — fall and restoration sudden,
         not gradual. History changes at once.
   4. Like second Greek view in that best was
      in beginning — but Hebrew fall is sudden
      rather than gradual.

In Pursuit of the Millenium (Sp?)

   D. 17th Century idea (up to modern times)
   1. Gradual progress can be brought about by
   man's own efforts. Man can achieve return to
   felicity by getting rid of evil — man, by
   taking things in his own hands, can change
   environment and change it from bad to
   perfect. [Note: God left out of this scheme.
   Man, not God, effects change.]

Idea of apocalypse (restoration of earth to perfection) a Hebrew one. Greeks looked at history as "everything repeats itself" or "things going from bad to worse" — Hebrew idea: beginning perfection, ending perfection, in between everything terrible — change from good to bad sudden and brought about by God. Modern idea (17th cent. on) man gradually brings about perfection by getting rid of evil in world.

FIGURE 4–3

Lecture Notes in 2–5–1 Format

Outline form — mainly sentence.

column. Without a clear grasp of such terms, concepts essential to an understanding of the subject may remain fuzzy. Every subject has its key terms. Learn them!

THE 2–6–2 FORMAT

Students who want more space than the 5-inch column provides often prefer the 2–6–2 format, which looks like this:

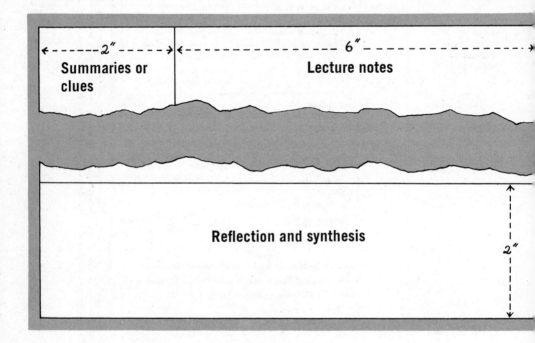

FIGURE 4–4

The 2–6–2 Format

This format appeals also to students who do not like to turn their notes sideways in order to write and read their summaries. Figure 4–5 shows the summary in a 2-inch space left for it at the bottom of the sheet.

THE 2–3–3–2 FORMAT

This scheme is often ideal for lectures which mainly explain and amplify the textbook. The sheet is ruled as shown in Figure 4–6.

Notes on the previously assigned textbook reading should be recorded first in the middle column. Then when taking lecture notes in the third

American Philosophy 333 — Sept. 23, 1960 — Prof. Murphy

What Am. Phil. is + what part it plays in Am. culture

1. Some terms + concepts :

Man's phil. — way he looks at and evaluates the world.
Philosophy — pursuit of truth — attempt to investigate reason or justification for our ultimate beliefs — push reason back as far as possible until we get at self-evident proofs. [see Collinwood on presuppositions]
Ultimate beliefs — are usually the influence of our times. As ideas chg., the traditional ideas are challenged. When challenges arise, then philosophies appear to find some fundamental truth — to bring truth into focus. Examine, adjust, throw out, chg. current thinking + beliefs.
Climate of beliefs — these are beliefs people hold without inquiry or investigation.

Assignment: Jonathan Edwards for Fri. 1st five selections — last 4 important. Suppl: H. Schneider, Hist. Am. Phil.

2. Jonathan Edwards — Calvinist theologian
   Doctrine: Absolute sovereignty of God — will + notion are predetermined by God. [Look up predestination]
   People started to think about free will. If God does everything, what can the human Will do? Nothing? Conflict!
   Edwards a conservative. Wanted to justify the established faith + bring into relation with current thought. Felt need of giving reasons for beliefs; didn't simply say "This is revealed".
   Example: When Jefferson severed connections with Britain, he gave reasons based on "self-evident" truths.   (more)→

Margin notes

Man's phil. — way he looks at life — based on daily experience
Phil. — Truth — based on principles
Definite relationship betw. culture + phil.
1. culture insecure
2. tensions arise
3. questions asked
4. phil. answers
Opinions of marketplace influence people

Edwards — Calvinist predeterminism
Is there Free Will?
To conserve estab. faith, Edwards gave basic reasons for faith

---

A country does not necessarily develop its culture according to an a priori set of philosophical principles. More likely the culture develops first, then philosophical principles are brought forth to support the culture. Furthermore, as the culture grows and changes, so do the philosophical principles which support it. ————————→

FIGURE 4–5

Lecture Notes in 2–6–2 Format: Paragraph Style

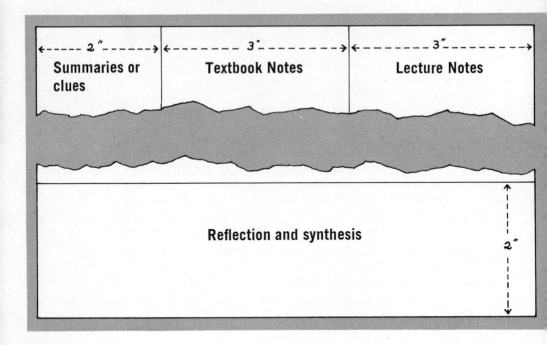

FIGURE 4–6

The 2–3–3–2 Format

column, you can avoid duplicating material you already have, but can add in the lecturer's explanations, examples, and supplementary comments. When you become accustomed to his ways you will be able to judge about how much extra space to leave between the items in column 2 in order to keep your lecture notes on the same points directly opposite them in column 3. In summarizing or "flagging," combine the two sets of notes so that in reciting you will synthesize them. Use the 2-inch space at the bottom of the sheet for a pre-examination summary, to pull together the two columns of notes in written form.

5

Reading Efficiently

College requires a lot of reading — more than you have ever done in your life. To make the most of your study hours you will need the ability to read rapidly, to adjust your rate of reading to the kind of materials you read and your purpose in reading them, and to understand thoroughly what you read. These are the skills of efficient reading. Happily for you, they are skills that you can develop by a conscious program of improvement, and this chapter will tell you how.

IMPROVING YOUR READING RATE

The ability to read *rapidly* is highly important to the college student. Habitual slowness cuts deeply into one's study time and actually interferes with comprehension. The key to efficient reading is learning to read words in groups, rather than one by one. Words mean little in themselves; they take on meaning in combination, in the context of a sentence. The faster you can convert words into facts and ideas, the more effectively you will read. When slow readers are trained to read faster, they find that their ability to concentrate improves greatly.

You may find at first, in developing good reading habits and correcting poor ones, that you *temporarily* sacrifice comprehension. As always, in breaking bad habits, there is likely to be a period of readjustment while you yield the imperfect skills you have in order to substitute better ones. But if you persist, and practice, the rewards will be great.

EYE FIXATIONS

Contrary to popular belief, the eyes of a good reader do not sweep across the page in a continuous motion. Eyes in motion do not see words clearly to read them. When you read, your eyes move across the page in a series of short, fast movements and longer pauses (fixations). It is the fixations that make up the bulk of the time spent in reading a page. When you take in several words during a fixation, you make fewer time-consuming pauses.

This is how a sentence looks to a word-by-word reader:

A / word / by / word / reader / is / a / slow / reader, / because / he / stops / to / photograph / each / word / separately.

But notice the difference if you look at phrases, or groups of words:

A reader / who takes in / groups of words / at each fixation / is a / fast reader. / He sees / more words / in half / the time.

Notice too that the meaning of this sentence comes through much more quickly and clearly when you read it in groups of words which naturally fit into "thought phrases." This is what good readers do.

If you are a slow reader, the chances are you read one word at a time. Here are some suggestions for training yourself to read in groups of words.

Practice taking in more than one word per eye fixation while reading the newspaper. Try making only two fixations to a column-line. You will find that your vision takes in words to the left and to the right of the focal point. The number of words you can see with one fixation is called your "span of recognition." After several days of practice, you will find that it is easy to take in two or three words at once. Research shows that more than three words at one fixation is rare.

When you have become proficient in controlling fixations while reading newspaper column-lines, try the longer lines of a book. Choose an interesting, easy book, such as a light novel, and practice reading groups of words for fifteen minutes each day.

Most readers, after completing one line, waste time by returning their eyes to the *first* word of the next line, thus taking in the entire left margin as well. To make better use of the span of recognition, the good reader returns to the *second* word in the next line.

(You can learn) (to return)

(your eyes) (rapidly and accurately)

(to the second) (word of the)

(next line.)

Another technique used by good readers is the *fast return sweep* from the end of one line to the second word of the next. This not only saves time but also seems to generate a psychological momentum which continues right through the reading of the line.

BAD HABITS TO OVERCOME

Vocalization. Extreme vocalization is the practice of audibly or sub-audibly pronouncing every word during reading, either by moving the lips or vocal chords or by thinking each word. The vocalizer is thus forced to read slowly, word by word, with the disadvantages which this involves.

To eliminate this habit some books advocate chewing gum or even clamping the jaws onto a pencil to keep the lips and tongue from moving. But such suggestions treat the symptoms and not the cause. The ideas presented above for improving your rate of reading through fixating groups of words and increasing the speed of the return sweep should help you break the vocalizing habit also. For if you achieve a high reading rate — one greater than the word-by-word vocalizing rate — it will be impossible for you to pronounce each word audibly or subaudibly.

Compulsive regression. Another block to rapid and efficient reading is the habit of regressing, going back a few words or lines to what has already been read. The root of the trouble is inattention. The reader's mind momentarily wanders; he sees words but doesn't really take them in. Then he realizes that he has missed something, and he looks back for it. Eventually a bad habit-pattern of backtracking becomes established.

Compulsive regression should not be confused with purposeful regression. A good reader often goes back to earlier lines or paragraphs to question, reflect, recall, or unravel a long, complex train of thought. You will never eliminate regression completely — nor should you. The problem is to overcome the habitual and pointless kind. For this purpose, use a 5 × 8-inch card to cover lines after you read them. Knowing that you can't go back forces you to get the meaning the first time. By moving the card rapidly, you can force yourself to read faster. Practicing to overcome regression while improving your reading rate is just another way of learning to concentrate.

Pointing. Moving along each line with a finger or a pencil pointing to each word is probably a habit held over from elementary school. It is a sure way to remain a word-by-word reader. To remove the underlying cause (fear of losing your place) hold a 5 × 8-inch card just above the line to be read; this will help you keep your eyes on the line. Unhampered by the pointing finger or pencil, the eyes can now take in words as groups instead of halting on each one. Soon you will gain confidence and be able to dispense with the card.

Head movements. A surprisingly large number of students keep their eyes fixed and move their heads from left to right when reading, instead of keeping the head still while the eyes move along the line in a series of fixations. This is not only inefficient but tiring, for the constant head movements can bring on muscular tension and headache. The habit is relatively easy to overcome, however. Place your book and your elbows on a desk or table; then nestle your chin in your cupped hands. In this way you will hold your head motionless and force your eyes to move across the page.

HOW FAST IS FAST?

The student who reads the newspaper, Plato's dialogues, a chemistry textbook, *Vanity Fair,* and *The Mystery of the Disappearing Corpse* all at the same speed is reading some things either too slow or too fast. Your rate of reading should be geared to your purpose in reading and to the kind of material being read. If you are reading for information you will go more slowly than you would if reading for entertainment. Slower reading is required for such purposes as note-taking, evaluating organizational structure, critical reading, following a logical argument, searching for implied meanings, or grasping details and amplifications of important ideas. A more rapid rate is more efficient for getting a general overview, searching for a specific item of information, or reviewing familiar material.

SKIMMING

Skimming is an invaluable tool. It can save you time and cut down on your reading load. Skimming is the technique for getting a general idea of what a book, article, or chapter is about without reading every word. It helps you decide whether you want to read a book thoroughly, whether it is repetitious of material you have already read, or whether it contains the specific information you are looking for.

How do you skim? Start by reading only the opening sentence of each paragraph. If it seems closely related to the subject or main idea in which you are interested, glance through the paragraph for key words and phrases and read the sentences in which they occur. Leaf through the pages in this way, reading carefully only those sections which contain pertinent information.

Skimming is also useful for locating specific information. Perhaps you want to pick out information about one person. Keep the person's name pictured in your mind and run down the lines looking for it. With practice you will find that particular combination of letters fairly leaping out of the page at you. Then you can read carefully the sentences or paragraphs in which the name appears. In the same way if you are skimming to find a date you can train your eyes to pass over other material and fix only on the dates.

IMPROVING YOUR COMPREHENSION

The ability to read rapidly is a useful skill, but only so far as it goes hand in hand with better understanding. We have seen that techniques for improving your reading rate also improve your comprehension by helping you to read in "thought phrases" and thus more readily to focus on information and ideas. In the remainder of this chapter we shall be concerned with techniques specifically centered on improved comprehension.

DISCERNING ORGANIZATIONAL PATTERN

As we saw in Chapter 3, every efficient writer organizes his material in a discernible pattern to make his points clear and understandable. Knowing the functions of the introduction, thesis, body, and conclusion, you can read better by keeping the following questions in mind.

1. *Introduction:*
   How does the author set the stage for his topic?
   What is unique? What is he emphasizing?
2. *Thesis:*
   What is the problem, issue, or topic?
3. *Body:*
   With what main ideas or information does the author support or develop his thesis?
   In what order does he present these materials? How in turn does he support *them?*
4. *Conclusion:*
   Does the author simply summarize?
   Or does he give additional information, interpretation, or insight?

Even in reading the newspaper you can make organizational pattern work for you. Most news stories follow the same pattern: the headline is the main point, the first paragraph is the topic paragraph and summary, and the rest of the story consists of amplifying details. Knowing this, you can cover a newspaper rapidly by reading headlines and first paragraphs, finishing only the stories of special interest to you.

GRASPING KEY IDEAS

A paragraph usually presents one key idea built around a "topic sentence" which is often, though not always, the opening sentence. Sometimes no one sentence serves this function; the main point must be gleaned from several sentences or inferred from the whole paragraph. Good readers look for and seize the key idea in each paragraph, whether it is stated or implied. To move from one key idea to another preserves continuity in reading and thus stimulates comprehension. A good reader also makes full use of signs pointing to important facts and concepts — signs such as "first" and "second," "1." and "*a,*" "most important" and "above all."

MAKING TRANSITIONAL WORDS WORK FOR YOU

Transitional words or phrases can often help you anticipate the next idea. They reveal the relationships among facts and ideas. And in so doing, they reveal the author's intention, the direction in which he is going and his evaluation of his materials. The following list shows how intention or relationship can be signaled by transitional words and phrases:

Intention or Relationship	Transitional Words and Phrases
Amplification	for example, in other words, that is
Cause and effect	accordingly, because, consequently, for this reason, hence, since, then, thus, therefore
Concession	accepting the data, granted that, of course
Contrast or change	but, conversely, despite, however, nevertheless, on the contrary, on the other hand, still, though, yet
Emphasis	above all, indeed, more important, to repeat
Equal value	at the same time, likewise, similarly
Increasing quantity	also, besides, furthermore, in addition, moreover, too
Order	finally, first, lastly, next, second, then
Summary	for these reasons, in brief, in conclusion, to sum up
Time	afterwards, before, formerly, later, meanwhile, now, presently, previously, subsequently, ultimately

DETECTING ATTITUDE OR TONE

Sometimes words *say* one thing but *mean* another. To comprehend and evaluate what you read, you must know whether the author is being serious and straightforward, satiric, sarcastic, ironic, or playful. In many cases, if you overlook the author's attitude, as expressed in the tone of his writing, you miss his intent or purpose.

A classic example of a piece of writing that "means" something quite different from what it "says" is Jonathan Swift's essay, "A Modest Proposal." Written in 1729, the "proposal" suggested that the desperate situation of the Irish people could be remedied by promoting a project for butchering and marketing the surplus children as delicacies for the table, "very proper for landlords, who, as they have already devoured most of the parents, seem to have the best titles to the children." To take the essay literally, as a hideous and inhuman proposal, is of course to miss the entire point: Swift's savage indignation on behalf of the Irish people, his hatred of injustice and inhumanity. Understanding that the tone is bitterly satiric, we can appreciate this essay as a great humane statement, intended to shock readers into awareness of an intolerable condition.

How do you know when to take a selection literally? There is no definite and easy way to tell. Sensitivity to attitude, intent, and tone is something you will acquire only through reading and analyzing. Start with known examples of satire, irony, humor, and so on, and look for words and phrases that provide clues. With practice you will develop an alert sense for what an author means beyond what he says.

NONVERBAL MATERIALS

Sizable portions of science and social science books are devoted to tables, graphs, diagrams, and pictures which convey a great deal of information. In many cases they are as important as the written word, yet many students give them no more than a passing glance.

Tables. Tables are used to present a large amount of factual information, usually statistics, in a compact, orderly arrangement that makes complex relationships immediately clear. For example, a table on the expectation of life and mortality at specified ages can show in a three-inch square that life expectancy varies with age race, sex, and occupation. The column headings list one set of "variables," and the side headings (stubs) another. The relationship between any two of these is shown at the intersection of a vertical and a horizontal column.

Graphs. Graphs, like tables, show relationships between two sets of variables. A line or curve graph also shows continuity; when the individual plotted points are connected, you can see and evaluate them in the context of past, present, and projected future.

Diagrams. In some science textbooks — zoology, for example — diagrams are used on almost every other page. A labeled diagram of an insect or of the internal structure of a frog helps one to visualize and understand the complex relationships of the parts. The student who studies by reproducing labeled diagrams from memory is the student who will know his subject.

Pictures. Pictures in a textbook are there because they have a job of teaching to do. They can help you visualize places, people, objects, situations; they can convey mood and tone. Don't merely glance at a picture; study it in relation to the text. If there is a caption, read it carefully. Try to see why the picture is used and how it is intended to deepen your understanding of the subject. A picture of a Greek temple can tell you a good deal about the mind of the ancient Greeks as expressed in their architecture. A photograph of an unusual rock formation can clarify a geological principle that you might not so fully grasp if it were presented in words alone.

THE VALUE OF BACKGROUND READING

Many writers assume that their readers share with them a common fund of knowledge, and allude to events, people, and literary or mythological characters without comment or explanation. Consider, for example, the following sentences: "And not long ago I was able to lay by my lantern, for

I found an honest man." The student with a good reading background immediately recognizes this reference to Diogenes, the ancient Greek Cynic philosopher who went about the streets in the daytime with a lighted lantern to satirize the difficulty of finding an honest man. The words "lantern" and "honest man," used together trigger an association which gives meaning to the sentence. The more the reader is able to bring to the words he reads, from his own experience or from other books, the more he gets out of them. Perhaps this is in part what Emerson had in mind when he said, " 'Tis the good reader makes the good book."

Finally, the more you read, the more you will enjoy reading. Most poor readers do not like to read, and because their reading is so limited, they do not improve in skill or in enjoyment. A personal reading program, over and beyond your course work, will enrich your background and increase both your reading skills and your enjoyment of books. In planning a program of reading, you might consult one or more of the following guides:

> *The Wonderful World of Books,* edited by Alfred Stefferud.
> *Books That Changed the World,* by Robert B. Downs.
> *A Guide to Basic Books,* by Booksellers Catalog Service, Inc.
> *The Lifetime Reading Plan,* by Clifton Fadiman.

These not only tell you about books but suggest titles, lists, and plans. Explore the field, consult your special interests, map out a course of action, and start reading. You will be pleasantly surprised at how quickly even fifteen minutes a day will yield results.

6

How to Read a Textbook

Textbooks serve several purposes. They may provide a framework for the course; enforce learning by stating again much that is said in class; clarify by saying the same thing in a different way; amplify by introducing other material; and they may sometimes interpret by presenting a point of view different from the instructor's. A textbook should therefore not be studied by itself or simply memorized. It should at every step be related to what is being done in class.

UNDERSTANDING THE AIMS OF A TEXTBOOK

The first step in using a textbook efficiently is to understand its methods. Read the preface, the introduction, if there is one, and the table of contents. These parts of a book can give you valuable insights into an author's ideas about his book. Here, within a very few pages, you can grasp his central theme or prime objective, stated simply and directly. (See Figure 6–1.)

The following, from the preface of a textbook on economics, states the author's point of view and admits his bias, and then gives you his "approach" to the subject.

> In addition to the importance of historical and institutional materials, I am convinced that a deliberate role should be given to *controversy* in introductory economics. All too often this is done, if at all, by presenting "both sides" to a question, and letting it go at that, leaving the student unstrung. I have not followed that procedure, but have allowed my own critical and positive views to emerge without inhibition. The reader may dispute my viewpoint at every turn, but I am convinced that the questions raised are important and that they merit serious examination. The good student of economics will learn something through honest and thorough dispute, even, perhaps particularly, with views he finds untenable. And he may thereby become more interested in the subject.[1]

[1] Douglas F. Dowd, *Modern Economic Problems in Historical Perspective* (rev. ed.; Ithaca, N.Y.: Norton Printing Co., 1960), preface.

In this volume I have aimed, within the available space, to represent as fully as possible the great literary critics from Aristotle to the present day, and then to supplement the selections with more abundant interpretation and commentary than is usually found. Where this book departs from existing anthologies, it does so, in the editor's opinion, in the following ways: It stresses some critics, particularly Hazlitt, whom other available collections have largely neglected. It represents some of the main critics since the Renaissance, especially Johnson, Coleridge, Arnold, and Eliot, much more copiously. There is no attempt to offer small excerpts, of a paragraph or a page or two, from a wide variety of writers. Instead, the editor has frankly reacted against the "snippet" kind of anthology.

Moreover, this volume tries, where possible, to offer complete selections. If separate chapters of books are counted, then forty-three of the eighty selections are complete units.

A final distinctive feature of this volume may be found in the amount and character of the commentary. Biographical and bibliographical information has been condensed and confined to notes.

In turning to the entire subject afresh, my intention in the commentary has been to approach literary criticism, first, through a concentrated focusing on major critics. Second, I have aimed to approach the subject through discussing the rise and development of historical trends in criticism. . . . Third, it has not seemed the smallest part of my editorial function to note, over and beyond their historical development, the general premises and implications that underlie or emerge from the various ways of approaching art.

Scope: Aristotle to present

How Different: Stress neglected critics; e.g. Hazlitt

Main critics more fully represented

No small excerpts

Complete selections

Distinctive: Notes

Aim of Commentary:
1. *Major critics*
2. *Historical trends in criticism*
3. *Definitions of art.*

FIGURE 6–1

The Function of a Preface

Much can be grasped about the scope, aims, and viewpoint of a book from its preface. The text is from the Preface to Criticism: The Major Texts *by Walter Jackson Bate, copyright, 1952, by Harcourt, Brace & World, Inc., and reprinted with their permission.*

The following paragraph, from the introduction to the same book, illustrates the author's use of "pre-outlining" to clarify the first chapter.

> In the following pages, we will examine the general features of capitalism, and go on to discuss some of the specific manifestations of American capitalism — something of its origins, the manner in which it has changed over time, and some of the leading tendencies now at work. We will examine, through the eyes of Karl Marx, how capitalism originated and developed; through the eyes of Adam Smith, we will examine the means by which a capitalist society is supposed to accomplish the end of social well-being.[2]

MENTAL PREPARATION

Effective reading takes concentration, and this may require some mental warming up. First, you might reflect on the importance and relation of the assignment to the whole pattern of the course. Make sure you know just what the assignment is, and review any comments your instructor may have made about it. (Form the habit in class of writing the assignment down exactly as the instructor gives it, together with full notes on anything he says about it.) If you are clear about the exact nature and purpose of the assignment, you will know what main points to look for as you read, and may be able to skip paragraphs or pages which are not relevant. In biology, for instance, you may be asked to learn the structure and life processes of an amoeba; in philosophy, the differences between the pragmatism of James and that of Peirce. Having these problems clearly in mind before you start reading makes it a good deal easier to find the answers.

Finally, before reading, ask yourself what you already know about the subject. The many landmarks already familiar to you will make it easier to get "the lay of the land."

SYSTEMATIC READING

Thorough, critical reading is easier if you develop the habit of reading systematically. Based in part on the SQ3R method developed by Professor F. P. Robinson,[3] the OK4R method described in the following pages employs some of the most effective techniques developed by psychologists of learning. The steps in this method are:

1. Get an Overview;
2. Determine Key Ideas;
3. Read;
4. Recall;
5. Reflect;
6. Review.

[2] *Ibid.*, p. 2.
[3] *Effective Study* (rev. ed.; New York: Harper and Brothers, 1961), pp. 29–30.

The OK4R Method of Reading

O   1. *Overview.* Take about five minutes to read introductory and summary paragraphs of the assignment. Then read center and side headings, or topic sentences if there are no headings, to determine general content and sequence of topics. Locate the main divisions.

K   2. *Key Ideas.* Distinguish key ideas from secondary ideas and supporting materials. Convert headings or topic sentences into questions — a sure way to become involved in the author's ideas.

R¹   3. *Read.* Read the sections or paragraphs consecutively to answer the questions you have formulated and to see how supporting materials reinforce key points. Pay close attention to transitional words and phrases. Keep asking yourself: What is the evidence? Does it prove the point? Is there enough support? Do I believe this? Why or why not?

R²   4. *Recall.* After reading, test your memory and understanding. Without looking at the book, try to say or write the main points and supporting materials in your own words. If you cannot do this immediately after reading, you cannot hope to tomorrow in class or next week in an examination.

R³   5. *Reflect.* Step 4, Recall, will help fix the material in your mind. To make it really yours, go further: think about it. Relating new facts and ideas to others you already know gives added meaning to new and old knowledge and establishes both more firmly in your mind. This is the essence of creative thinking: the discovery of new relationships and new significance.

R⁴   6. *Review.* To keep material fresh in mind, review it periodically. Re-read your notes and say over the sequence of main ideas and supporting materials until you have them once more firmly in mind. Mastery is a never-ending process.

Using the OK4R System

1. *Overview.* Much can be learned in five minutes of overview. Reading introductory and concluding paragraphs, center and side headings, and topic sentences yields a quick impression of aim, coverage, and specific ideas. Note how much can be gleaned by reading only the first sentence of the paragraph in Figure 6–2. Getting an overview is like climbing a hill from which you can view the forest before starting to pick your way through the trees. It also helps you to concentrate better on a thorough reading.

2. *Key ideas.* Headings, such as "Mental Differences among Races" and "The Concept of Pure Races," tell you what the author is writing about, but not what he has to say. Ideas are the topics *plus* what the author says about them: e.g., "The concept of pure races *is not scientifically defensible*," or

Harlem, physically at least, has changed very little in my parents' lifetime or in mine. Now as then the buildings are old and in desperate need of repair, the streets are crowded and dirty, there are too many human beings per square block. Rents are 10 to 58 per cent higher than anywhere else in the city; food, expensive everywhere, is more expensive here and of an inferior quality; and now that the war is over and money is dwindling, clothes are carefully shopped for and seldom bought. Negroes, traditionally the last to be hired and the first to be fired, are finding jobs harder to get, and, while prices are rising implacably, wages are going down. All over Harlem now there is felt the same bitter expectancy with which, in my childhood, we awaited winter: it is coming and it will be hard; there is nothing anyone can do about it.

FIGURE 6-2

The Function of a Topic Sentence

In this paragraph from James Baldwin, Notes of a Native Son *(Boston: Beacon Press, 1955), p. 57, notice particularly the following: (1) the topic sentence — here, the opening sentence — which states the subject of the paragraph; (2) the examples which support the topic sentence; (3) the final sentence, which rounds off the paragraph by referring back to the topic sentence.*

"The concept of pure races *was used by the Nazis as a brutal political weapon*." It is as important to know what the author says about his topic as to know what the topic is.

3. *Read.* It is not enough to grasp key ideas; it is necessary also to discover what supporting ideas and facts are used to develop them. As you read, you should continually ask, "Why — or how — is this true?" For example, the topic sentence (main idea) of the paragraph in Figure 6–2 is, "Harlem, physically at least, has changed very little in my parents' lifetime or in mine." With this idea firmly in mind you should ask, "What is the evidence for this statement?" Asking questions and finding answers is a stimulating intellectual exercise and an aid to understanding.

Read for facts, ideas, and relationships — in short, for *sense*. Make full use of organizational clues. If a sentence or paragraph begins "On the one hand," watch for the inevitable "On the other hand," which introduces the other side of the argument. Innocent little everyday words like "as," "since," "because," and "although" are as important in relating parts of a thought as a plus, minus, or square root sign is in a math problem. Ignoring or misreading them can get you in serious trouble. (See Figure 6–3.)

In following an author's development of his thought, keep his aim in mind. If you lose the thread, turn back to his introduction or his statement of his thesis, or look ahead to his conclusion, to get a better idea of where you are.

If you get bogged down in a really difficult sentence or paragraph, here is a method which some students find helpful. Read the material without the appositives and other modifying phrases, to avoid getting lost in a maze of language. When the framework, shows clearly through, so that you can grasp the main idea or fact, then you can go back and read the material with all its "trimmings" to get the full sense.

<u>On the one hand</u> there are the traditional <u>acts and observances,</u> regarded by the natives as sacred, carried out with reverence and awe, hedged around with prohibitions and special rules of behavior. <u>Such</u> acts and observances are always associated with beliefs in supernatural forces, especially those of magic, <u>or</u> with ideas about beings, spirits, ghosts, dead ancestors, or gods. <u>On the other hand,</u> a moment's reflection is sufficient to show that no art or craft however primitive could have been invented or maintained, no organized form of hunting, fishing, tilling, or search for food could be carried out without the careful observation of natural process and a firm belief in its regularity, without the power of reasoning and without confidence in the power of reason; <u>that is,</u> without the rudiments of science.

FIGURE 6–3

The Function of Transitional Words

A good reader makes use of words and phrases providing clues to transitions and relationships, such as those underlined here in this paragraph from Bronislaw Malinowski, Magic, Science and Religion and Other Essays *(New York: Doubleday and Company, Inc., 1948), pp. 17–18.*

If you are taking notes on your reading, you are ready to do so only when you have thoroughly assimilated the material and can condense the essence of it in your own words. (See Chapter 7.)

4. *Recall.* When you have finished reading, you are ready for the second R — Recall. Recalling what you have read forces you to test your understanding. It spotlights not only what you failed to remember, but what you failed to grasp.

As an aid to recall, you may want to mark your textbook for key ideas and other important information, as described later in this chapter. Or if you have been taking notes on your reading, now is the time to reinforce them with recall clues (see Chapter 7).

Another way to assist recall is to picture in your mind's eye concepts and facts which can be visualized — e.g., diagrammed mathematical, physical, or sociological relationships; a subtle color change during a chemical reaction; a dramatic moment in history.

If you will test yourself with the techniques of recall when you complete a reading assignment, you will know what you know — and what you don't know — while you still have time to do something about it.

5. *Reflect.* Professor Alfred North Whitehead, philosopher and mathematician, spoke about the knowledge which grows out of throwing ideas "into fresh combination." He was referring to speculation, projecting one's thoughts beyond familiar experience, considering new knowledge and ideas in the light of old, and old in the light of new. Reflection means investigating the implications of ideas, following up insights, asking questions, noting reservations. Reflections should not be left vague, but should be pursued until ideas take definite shape. If you need more information, an encyclopedia or a standard book on the subject will often give you what you need to bring fuzzy ideas into focus.

Students who do not think about what they have read miss the opportunity to gain real grasp of principles. Many students who can spout facts find it hard to apply these facts to unfamiliar situations or use them in new combinations. Manipulating facts — reflecting upon them — makes them yours as nothing else can. When different authors hold diverging opinions try to see why each believes as he does. Think through the problem from the viewpoint of each, and be alert to see where one or the other departs from the facts, overemphasizes some facts at the expense of others, or places a different interpretation on the facts. What do you think is the proper balance?

Reflection is a skill that you can take with you wherever you go and make use of in spare moments. It can be carried on while walking from one building to another, standing in line, waiting for a friend, or riding a bus. Men who have made great discoveries have reported that some of their best insights came in unlikely places and at odd times.

The subconscious plays an important role in creative thinking and discovery. We have all had an exciting idea or even the solution to a problem suddenly flash upon us at a moment when we have apparently not been thinking about it. The subconscious continues to work on concepts introduced deeply enough into the mind through reflection.

6. *Review.* Reviewing is the final step in effective reading. True reviewing is not just "looking over" lecture and reading notes. It is an active process of trying to remember, without prompting, what has already been learned. From time to time, go back over a section of your textbook or your reading notes, practice recalling as much as you can, then look again at book or notes to see where you were right, where you made mistakes, and what you left out. Continue recalling and verifying until you master the material.

To vary the process, put yourself in the instructor's place. What would you ask if you were giving a test? Write out three or four questions which you believe cover the main issues, then answer them. You will be surprised how often these same questions come up in quizzes and exams. This is not out-guessing the instructor; this is studying to learn.

HOW TO MARK A TEXTBOOK

Have you ever seen a scholar's well-worn copy of a favorite book? A book he cherishes usually bears his mark — notes which have deep significance for him, underlinings, papers slipped between pages, cross references — "compare p. 234" — and an array of other favorite symbols.

A book well marked becomes very much your own. You may underline words and phrases which are the essence of the main ideas. Some people use a double underline for main ideas and a single underline for important supporting ideas. Beware of underlining too much. When three or more consecutive lines seem worth underlining, use a vertical bracket at the outer margin instead. An asterisk may be used to stress particularly important ideas. Some people box or circle key terms, or words of enumeration and transition.

You may also wish to make concise summary notes in the margins. These should be brief yet full enough to serve later as clues for recall, reflection, and review. Numbers written above words or in margins opposite underlined portions show series of ideas, arguments, steps, or facts. A question mark beside lines you do not understand serves as a healthy reminder to clear up the point with another student or with your instructor. When you disagree with the author, you can write "disagree" in the margin or develop a symbol of your own to express the same idea.

Record insights — the kind that pop into your mind while you read — in the top or bottom margins, or on small sheets of paper which may be inserted between pages. Re-reading these notes during review sessions may help you recapture other associations previously made, thus deepening your understanding.

A word of warning is in order, however. Textbook marking can be a useful aid to study and review, but it must be done with thought and care. Otherwise it can become mere busy-work — just another dodge to avoid genuine recall, reflection, and review. Drawing underlines and boxes, inserting symbols and question marks, can give you a false sense of accomplishment when in fact you are not thinking deeply about what you read. Then, too, if you over-mark your book, you defeat the purpose of quick identification of important points, and when you come to re-read you will find yourself deciphering a code instead. Finally, the "you" that marks the book will not be quite the same "you" that reviews it. You grow in knowledge; many of the things it seemed so important to underscore, box, circle, star, question, comment on, or disagree with in October or November will be accepted and commonplace by January or June, and your earlier marks may only hamper your later re-reading. Use the aid that marking your text can give you, by all means; just don't go overboard.

Examples of Marked Textbook Pages. Following are four specimens from different subject areas, showing how the marking techniques in the chapter may be used — or abused.

The first example (Figure 6–4) is far too heavily marked. It is crammed with single and double underlines, brackets, asterisks, boxes, marginal notes, numbers above words, question marks, disagreements, summaries, words and ideas to look up, and more. So much marking is not only a waste of time; trying to emphasize too much, it actually emphasizes nothing. And it makes re-reading almost impossible.

The second example (Figure 6–5), another page from the same animal physiology text, shows more reasonable markings, which quickly guide the eye to the main line of the discussion. The marginal note expands the heading to a quick summary.

The third example (Figure 6–6) is from a history text. Since dates are important, this student associated the time of the Crusades with a date he knew — 1492. Notice also the summary notes in the margin and the circles representing concepts and geographical locations the student wanted to look up. The mysterious-looking "11C" is his abbreviation for "eleventh century."

The fourth example (Figure 6–7) is from a novel, Herman Melville's *Moby-Dick.* It is seldom necessary to mark a novel in the same way as an expository textbook, but striking and significant clues to character, event, or interpretation may be specially marked. It is a good idea to list marked pages on the flyleaf for easy reference, ideally with a clue, which in this case might be: "page 51, Ahab's scar — a symbol?"

Summary: Color vision a puzzle. No proof all people see same thing. Chickens & bees can see some colored lights and not others. Bees, men, monkeys, turtles, lizards, birds and teleost fish can distinguish colors — other animals cannot.

(Marginal notes, left column:)

I. Color vision in people.
  A. Can't explain how we see color
  B. All shades matched through mixing primary colors
  C. No proof all people see color in same way — assume they do — can't assume with animals

Disagree? what kind of proof is needed that all people experience color in same way? If all people call something red, isn't that proof?

II. Color vision in animals.
  A. Can animals see light of a given color?
    1. – chickens
    2. – honeybees
  B. Can animals distinguish color?
    1. – bees can distinguish colors
    2. other animals which can

Look up:
m μ
teleost fish
elasmobranch fish

Color Vision in Animals

Color vision is extremely puzzling to the physiologist; we have no satisfactory theory of color vision, nor can we explain how we see color. For example, we cannot explain why we see white light if we mix spectrally pure red (656 mμ) and blue-green (492 mμ), or why the sensation of spectral green can be perfectly matched by a mixture of yellow and blue. We do know, however, that all shades of color can be matched by appropriate mixtures of three so-called primary colors: red, yellow, and blue. A deviating color vision, known as color blindness, is associated with reduced acuity for shades of green or red (or both). It is quite common in man, occurring in about 8 per cent of all males and 0.6 per cent of females.

From our own experience, each of us knows that he sees colors and that these colors have names, and by inference we assume (although we have no proof) that when somebody says "red" he has the same experience we have. Such inference, however, is completely unjustified when it comes to animals of a different species, with whom we cannot talk; but even so, we can discover some facts about color vision in animals. We really want the answers to two questions; first, whether an animal can see light of a given color at all and, secondly, whether different colors are perceived differently so that they can be distinguished.

Some simple tests can often answer our first question. If a chicken is fed in a darkroom that has rice grains scattered on the floor and the grains are illuminated with spectral colors, the animals will pick up all the grains in red, yellow, and green light, but not the ones in blue light, although these are clearly visible to us. Evidently the chicken eye is not able to perceive blue as light. In a similar fashion we can show that honeybees are insensitive to red, and, by using red light, we can observe their life in the "darkness" inside the hive without disturbing them. On the other hand, bees are sensitive to ultraviolet, which we do not see.

Our second question — can animals distinguish colors? — has been answered by training experiments. If, for example, bees are trained to feed from a dish of sugar solution placed on a yellow disk, they will rapidly learn to seek food on a yellow background. If the full dish is now placed on a blue background and an empty dish on the yellow, the bees will continue seeking food on the yellow background. With a careful application of this and other training experiments, we are able to show that bees can distinguish colors (although we do not know *what* they see). In similar ways, it has been shown that at least some teleost fishes can discriminate colors, but elasmobranchs cannot. Turtles, lizards, and birds have color vision, but most mammals, except man and monkeys, are unable to discriminate color.

FIGURE 6–4

Marking a Textbook: Over-marking

In trying to emphasize too much, the student who marked this page defeated his purpose. The text is reprinted from Knut Schmidt-Nielsen, Animal Physiology (© 1960. Prentice-Hall, Inc., Englewood Cliffs, N.J.), pp. 81–82; by permission.

The Homing of the Salmon

Some time after a young salmon is hatched in a fresh-water stream, it follows the river system down to the ocean, where it spends several years and grows rapidly into a mature fish of considerable size. During the years in the ocean, the salmon travels over great distances, but when it returns to fresh water to spawn, it always goes back to the stream where it was born. How it finds its way back to the same stream, several years after leaving it, has been one of the great mysteries of biology. To confirm that salmon *do* return to the stream of their birth, thousands of young salmon have been marked as they descend to a river's mouth, and then checked upon their re-entry. In one of the largest studies ever made, Canadian investigators marked 469,326 young sockeye salmon in the Fraser River. Over the following years, nearly 11,000 of these were recovered in that river as they returned from the ocean, but not one single marked fish was ever found to have strayed into another stream. How do they find their way back from wanderings that take them hundreds and hundreds of miles out to sea? And they don't even seem to enter another river to check if one of its tributaries could be the right place.

The riddle of the migrating salmon is slowly being unraveled by careful physiological studies, and it now appears that the sense of smell guides the fish back to its home stream. Fishes have an extremely sensitive chemoreceptive sense and can learn to distinguish many "odors."

to native stream by smell

FIGURE 6–5

Marking a Textbook: Effective Marking

Reasonable markings guide the eye to the main line of the discussion. The text is reprinted from Knut Schmidt-Nielsen, Animal Physiology (© 1960. Prentice-Hall, Inc., Englewood Cliffs, N.J.), pp. 89–90; by permission.

The Crusades

1096 –
to late
13 C –
and 200 yrs.
before
Columbus

From the time when they occurred to the present, the crusades have commanded public attention and called forth innumerable chronicles, histories long and short, and even poems. Their place in the historiographical tradition of Europe is thus assured, and the very word crusade has become familiar in our vocabulary. But if <u>historians,</u> mediaeval and modern, have <u>agreed</u> that the crusades were <u>interesting and important,</u> they have <u>differed</u> widely in explaining their <u>origins</u> and interpreting their <u>significance.</u> Indeed, it might be questioned whether they belong in a discussion of the mediaeval church. They were, however, <u>launched originally by the papacy;</u> and the <u>church's role,</u> though it diminished, was <u>never negligible.</u> In this brief account it will be possible only to summarize the more generally accepted conclusions.

Causes
1. Seljuks

<u>First,</u> it is clear that the <u>eight large expeditions</u> from 1096 to the <u>later</u> years of the <u>thirteenth</u> century, as well as the many less important ventures, were <u>occasioned by</u> the political and military <u>successes of Islam.</u> <u>In particular,</u> they were a response to a comparatively new menace presented in the second half of the eleventh century by the <u>Seljuk Turks.</u> The Seljuks had overrun the Bagdad caliphate and as a consequence of a resounding victory over a Byzantine army

Manzikert

at <u>Manzikert in 1071</u> opened the way to the conquest of Asia Minor. <u>Byzantium</u> had faced Islam across the straits before, but never had it <u>lost the entire hinterland of Asia Minor.</u>

2. 11 C
energy;
Cluny;

expansion

<u>Second,</u> the crusades were <u>made possible</u> by the religious, political, and economic <u>energy</u> so characteristic <u>of the eleventh century.</u> The Cluny reform reached a climax in the second half of the century, and it was not difficult for an ecclesiastically militant church to direct its forces to the military defense of Christendom and the recovery of the Holy City, Jerusalem. <u>Politically and economically,</u> eleventh-century Europe was entering one of those <u>periods of expansion</u> which have characterized its civilization down to modern times.

FIGURE 6–6

Marking a Textbook: Effective Marking

Notice the use of marginal summary notes and the circling of important terms and concepts the student wanted to look up. The text is reprinted from Marshall W. Baldwin, The Medieval Church (Ithaca, N.Y.: Cornell University Press, 1953), pp. 98–99.

tone

behind us. It was one of those less <u>lowering</u>, but still grey and gloomy enough mornings of the transition, when with a fair wind the ship was rushing through the water with a <u>vindictive</u> sort of leaping and <u>melancholy</u> rapidity, that as I mounted to the deck at the call of the forenoon watch, so soon as I levelled my glance towards the taffrail, foreboding shivers ran over me. Reality outran <u>apprehension;</u> Captain <u>Ahab</u> stood upon his quarter-deck.

There seemed no sign of common bodily illness about him, nor of the recovery from any. He looked like a man cut away from the stake, when the fire has overrunningly wasted all the limbs without consuming them, or taking away one particle from their compacted aged robustness. His whole high, broad form, seemed made of solid bronze, and shaped in an unalterable mould, like Cellini's cast Perseus. Threading its way out from among his grey hairs, and continuing right down one side of his tawny scorched face and neck, till it disappeared in his clothing, you saw a slender <u>rod-like mark, lividly whitish.</u> It resembled that perpendicular seam sometimes made in the straight, lofty trunk of a great tree, when the upper <u>lightning</u> tearingly darts down it, and without wrenching a single twig, peels and grooves out the bark from top to bottom, ere running off into the soil, leaving the <u>tree still greenly alive, but branded.</u> Whether that mark was born with him, or whether it was the scar left by some desperate wound, no one could certainly say. By some tacit consent, throughout the voyage little or no allusion was made to it, especially by the mates. But once Tashtego's senior, an old Gay-Head Indian among the crew, superstitiously asserted that not till he was full forty years old did Ahab become that way branded, and then it came upon him, not in the fury of any mortal fray, but in an elemental strife at sea. Yet, this wild hint seemed inferentially negatived, by what a grey <u>Manxman insinuated,</u> an old sepulchral man, who, having never before sailed out of Nantucket, had never ere this laid eye upon wild Ahab. Nevertheless, the old sea-traditions, the immemorial credulities, popularly invested this old Manxman with preternatural powers of discernment. So that no white sailor seriously contradicted him when he said that if ever Captain Ahab should be tranquilly laid out—which might hardly come to pass, so he muttered—then, whoever should do that last office for the dead, would find a <u>birth-mark on him from crown to sole.</u>

scar – symbol

FIGURE 6-7

Marking a Novel Used as a Text: Melville's Moby-Dick

7

Taking Notes on Textbook

and Library Readings

The first reason for taking notes on reading is the same as for taking notes on lectures: to have a complete and permanent record of the course materials for study and review. But, you may say, you see the need for lecture notes, because you can't go back to the heard lecture unless you have made a record of it; but since you *can* go back to the printed page, why take notes?

For one thing, you can't always go back to the book. A great deal of your reading will be done in library books which will not always be available just when you want them for review. More important, however, note-taking is more than making a record. It is a creative part of the reading and study process described in Chapter 6. Good notes are central to active, systematic reading and to the important work of recall, reflection, and review.

If you have marked your textbook thoughtfully, as discussed on pages 46–47, these markings will serve you as notes. However, you can only mark books you own. In advanced courses, particularly, much if not most of your reading will be done from library sources. Some students, moreover, prefer to take notes instead of marking their own textbooks. For all these reasons, it is important to develop early in your college career this essential skill of taking notes on what you read.

SOME SUGGESTED FORMATS

There is really no one best set-up for notes. The suggestions made here — gleaned from the experience of hundreds of students — are to help you develop the forms and procedures that work most effectively for you. You will find it convenient, however, to adopt the general format already recommended for lecture notes: a $8\frac{1}{2} \times 11$-inch sheet of notebook paper, ruled vertically to provide a wide column at the right for your reading notes and a narrow column at the left for recall clues (a 2–6 format). When the lectures follow the textbook closely, the 2–3–3–2 format described in Chapter 4 (pages 28–30) is useful for combining reading and lecture notes.

RECORDING NOTES

After your overview of the material (Step 1 of the OK4R reading method, page 42), and your identification of key ideas (Step 2, page 42), you are ready to begin a close paragraph-by-paragraph reading (Step 3, page 43). You must read each paragraph through carefully to understand, extract, summarize, and record its essence.

Subjects which deal mainly with factual material demand an enumeration of facts, principles, or rules. For example, your geology notes might look like those shown in Figure 7–1.

With material that deals more with ideas and their relationships than with facts, you will be reading for concepts and theories that are likely to span many paragraphs. The skimming you did in your overview will have given you an idea of what the main concepts are and how extensively they are treated. Your task then is to summarize and condense many paragraphs into one or two. In the notes shown in Figure 7–2 several paragraphs of reading have been boiled down into relatively few words.

When a highly condensed résumé of a chapter, selection, or book is needed, the organizational pattern system — based on Introduction-Thesis-Body-Conclusion, as described in Chapter 3 — is useful in forcing you to understand clearly the author's thesis and the way he develops and supports it. Figure 7–3 is an example of this. Here a one-inch column has been provided at the right for synthesis and reflection.

Notes need not follow a formal outline or any other complicated scheme. One of the most efficient ways of taking notes is to condense a paragraph or other unit of information into one meaningful sentence, with an appropriate heading or catchword. Important new terms should be defined briefly and key words may be underlined.

RECALL CLUES   NOTES ON CHAPTER

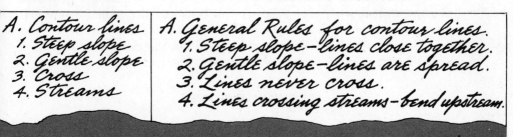

A. Contour lines   A. General Rules for contour lines.
1. Steep slope   1. Steep slope – lines close together.
2. Gentle slope   2. Gentle slope – lines are spread.
3. Cross   3. Lines never cross.
4. Streams   4. Lines crossing streams – bend upstream.

FIGURE 7–1

Reading Notes on Material Emphasizing Facts:
Enumeration

RECALL CLUES	NOTES ON CHAPTER

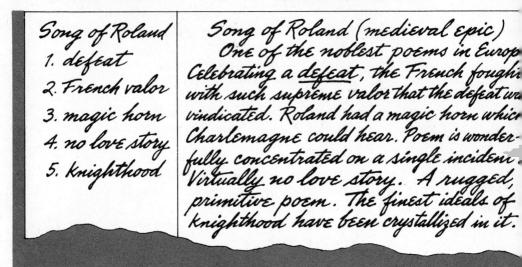

Song of Roland
1. defeat
2. French valor
3. magic horn
4. no love story
5. knighthood

Song of Roland (medieval epic)
One of the noblest poems in Europe
Celebrating a _defeat_, the French fought
with such supreme valor that the defeat was
vindicated. Roland had a magic horn which
Charlemagne could hear. Poem is wonder-
fully concentrated on a single incident.
Virtually no love story. A rugged,
primitive poem. The finest ideals of
knighthood have been crystallized in it.

FIGURE 7–2

*Reading Notes on Material Emphasizing Ideas and Relationships:
Summary and Condensation*

You must constantly fight the impulse to "copy" the reading instead of taking notes on it. Simply transferring blocks of material, word for word, from the text to your notebook defeats the purpose of note-taking. For part of the value of taking notes is to make sure you understand what you have read and can summarize it in your own words, picking out the main points and ignoring the unimportant details. Copying, moreover, yields notes too voluminous to be useful for study and review.

At first, note-taking may seem a tedious drag on your reading. It is true that the student who takes no notes will complete his reading assignment sooner than the note-taker, but he will have no aids for future reference, and he will have missed the opportunity to think out the material as one reads and to restate it in one's own words for maximum understanding.

REMEMBERING NOTES

When you have read and comprehended the assignment and summarized the central points, you are ready to practice the *active recall* which will convert facts and concepts into knowledge you can retain and use (Step 4 of the OK4R method, page 45). Read over your notes to be sure they say what you mean and are clear enough to mean the same thing weeks and even months later. Write summarizing notes and recall clues in the 2-inch

Phil. 313 – American Philosophy.
Henry David Thoreau, 1817–1862. _Walden; or Life in the Woods._ (1854)   Nov. 9, 1959.

I. Introduction

Experiment in living close to nature.

   Thoreau voluntarily withdrew from a civilization which he felt was getting too complicated. He spent 2 yrs., 2 mos., and 2 days living at Walden Pond to regain the simplicity of life which comes when one lives close to the soil.

II. Thesis

Each man should pause to decide just how he should spend his life. Is he paying too dearly for unessentials?

   In a complex civilization, the fast flowing current of unessentials stemming from custom, tradition, advertising, etc., somehow sweeps a man away from the genuine goals in life.

   Only by temporarily cutting oneself off from civilization, could man realize that his life need not be so complex. By getting back to nature to rethink the basic issues of life, man could chart his course, and attempt to steer his life in accordance with these standards (not the expediences set up by the pressures of complex civilization).

III. Body

   Thoreau did not wish to hold up progress or civilization; rather, he wished that man would be more contemplative and selective in his actions.

Man should awaken and become aware of real life.

Live simply & you will live more fully.

   Thoreau chronicled his experiences at Walden Pond. He wanted to become familiar with nature.
   a. He built his own hut.
   b. Average cost of living a week was 27 cents.
   c. He observed nature: trees, birds, animals, etc.

   He believed that every man ought to measure up to the best he could do. What the best is, depends upon the individual. To have a standard to measure up does not mean that all must have the same, but every man should measure up to a standard in the best way he is able to.

IV. Summary

Urged people to reject unessentials, and get back to fundamentals.

   Thoreau wanted to demonstrate that many so-called necessities were not necessary at all. He wanted man to observe, appreciate, and evaluate what was important in life. Once man had set his sights upon the good life, he should follow it without compromising.

Complex civilization has caused man to lose sight of life's fundamental goals. Only in the quietness of nature can man recognize his errors, rethink the problem, determine his new actions, and thereby regain his spiritual equilibrium.

FIGURE 7–3

_Reading Notes in the Form of a Highly Condensed Summary:
Organizational Pattern System_

column. Now study a section of your notes at a time; cover it with your hand or a piece of paper, and from the clues try to recall the section, reciting aloud or even writing it out; then look again at your notes to see what errors you made or what you forgot; then repeat the process until you can successfully reproduce the material. This is the same process recommended for effective study of lecture notes (page 25).

Finally, a word about studying and taking notes on maps, charts, diagrams, and tables. Such materials are not window-dressing; they are an important part of the text and convey information which either supplements or explains it. A map of a military campaign, a chart showing how the average dollar is spent, a diagram illustrating how distances are measured by triangulation, a table giving figures on increase in population — all these should be studied and, if important enough, sketched into your notebook. These nonverbal notes, just like your verbal notes, should be studied by the process of recall, as described above. In biology, for example, one sure way of memorizing the structure of the amoeba is to sketch it, labeling its parts and properties until you can easily reproduce it, by recall, to look something like Figure 7–4.

There is no better way to prepare for an examination than by training yourself so thoroughly in the technique of active recall that you can reproduce your notes without looking at them.

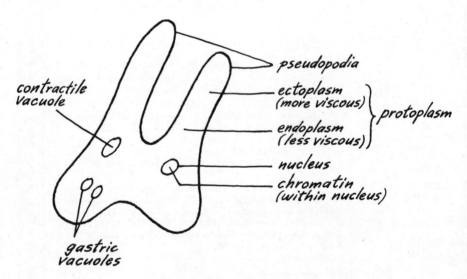

FIGURE 7–4

Diagramming as a Study Aid: The Structure of the Amoeba

8

The Importance of Vocabulary

The close relation between vocabulary and academic performance is suggested by a survey, in an eastern engineering college, which showed that the students who improved most in vocabulary during their freshman year averaged three or four places nearer the top of their class during the sophomore year, whereas those who did not improve at all in vocabulary averaged 7.5 places nearer the bottom.[1] The Human Engineering Laboratory, which specializes in testing business executives, has found a significant correlation between high vocabulary scores and success at the top executive level. These and similar findings demonstrate that a good vocabulary is not only the mark of an educated man or woman but a valuable asset both in college and after.

LEARNING WORDS AS CONCEPTS

Throughout your college years new words will flood into your consciousness. Because many of these new words are the keys to ideas and information, they are at the very heart of learning. When students get into difficulties in their courses, the trouble can often be traced back to the imperfect notions they have of terms which are essential to an understanding of subject matter. A first-year science course, for example, may introduce almost as many new words as a first course in a foreign language. In chemistry you will meet such words as *kinetic, colloid, adsorption, isomer,* and *osmosis;* in biology, *symbiosis, chromosome, pseudopod, haploid;* in geology, *syncline, moraine, diastrophic, Pleistocene;* in psychology, *holistic, synapses, receptor, mesomorph;* in sociology, *ecology, ethnocentrism, superorganic, mana;* and so on. Then there are words like *base* in chemistry and *accommodation* in psychology, which may not literally be new to you but which have specific meanings in certain subjects and therefore must be learned like new words. For the college student a wide vocabulary is not just something "nice" to have, because it is a cultural asset; it is a necessary tool for grasping fundamental ideas and facts.

[1] Cited in *Word Study,* copyright 1958 by G. & C. Merriam Co., Publishers of the Merriam-Webster Dictionaries.

AWARENESS OF WORDS

Many of the new words you meet will not, of course, be essential keys to ideas or concepts. Some words refine, qualify, enrich, or expand a thought but are not central to it. Consider the two following sentences:

> It has been suggested that since reef-building corals are well-provided with symbiotic algae, they may be actually dependent on those algae and cannot thrive at depths where the algae fail to get enough light for photosynthesis.[2]

> Numerous photographs of the great actress, with affectionate inscriptions, were displayed about the drawing-room, and other souvenirs of their life together adorned the little tables and *étagères*.[3]

If you don't know the meaning of *symbiotic, algae,* and *photosynthesis,* you simply cannot understand the first sentence, for these are key terms, essential to the meaning. On the other hand, you don't need to know what *étagères* are to understand the second sentence. You can assume from the context that an *étagère* is a piece of furniture of some kind, and comprehension is not impeded. Especially in literary and narrative writing, context often provides an adequate working clue, though as you develop sensitivity to words you will want to follow them up to verify the apparent contextual meanings.

People who have a rich vocabulary don't just memorize a lot of words. They notice new words when they read or hear them. They distinguish between key terms, which stand for key ideas, and words that can be figured out from the context but are not absolutely essential to its meaning. They learn to discriminate among different meanings of the same word. They tend to be interested in the roots and histories of words. In short, they have an *awareness* of words, and this is the most important quality for vocabulary building.

One way to develop this awareness or sensitivity is to read good writing. As George William Curtis, a master of style, said, "Bathe yourself in good discourse." You can also study words directly. This chapter suggests some practical techniques for direct word study as a means of expanding the frontiers of your vocabulary.

TEST YOUR VOCABULARY

As a warm-up exercise, test yourself on the vocabulary quiz (opposite) prepared by the publishers of the Merriam-Webster dictionaries. The phrases on this list were taken from books, magazines, and newspapers at the level of reading at which the college student is expected to be competent.

[2] Gairdner B. Moment, *General Zoology* (Boston: Houghton Mifflin Company, 1958), p. 111.
[3] Thomas Mann, "Mario and the Magician."

TEST YOUR VOCABULARY

DIRECTIONS: Underline the one of the five word choices which most nearly expresses the meaning of the italicized word in the phrase in the left-hand column.

(Answers are given on page 65.)

1. An *inscrutable* face — 1. jovial 2. inexpressive 3. frightened 4. distinguished 5. emaciated
2. *Bemused* by his message — 1. dazed 2. threatened 3. instructed 4. disturbed 5. reassured
3. To *deride* a suggestion — 1. make 2. discuss 3. adopt 4. ridicule 5. disregard
4. *Perjured* testimony — 1. judicial 2. forceful 3. objective 4. false 5. frightening
5. A *diminution* of tensions — 1. decrease 2. stabilization 3. creation 4. increase 5. prevention
6. *Turbid* water — 1. limpid 2. sterilized 3. cloudy 4. lukewarm 5. cold
7. A *turgid* stream — 1. rippling 2. roaring 3. swirling 4. flowing 5. swollen
8. *Mundane* affairs — 1. religious 2. illegal 3. business 4. recreational 5. worldly
9. A *burgeoning* population — 1. growing 2. hungry 3. discontented 4. bilingual 5. creative
10. Exposed to *calumny* — 1. disease 2. hardships 3. slander 4. treatment 5. travail
11. *Somnolent* students — 1. intelligent 2. youthful 3. drowsy 4. forgetful 5. matriculated
12. *Redoubtable* advisors — 1. respected 2. senile 3. weak 4. international 5. unconcerned
13. A *maladroit* candidate — 1. astute 2. awkward 3. studious 4. experienced 5. egocentric
14. A *sententious* oration — 1. clever 2. spellbinding 3. fascinating 4. hypocritical 5. pompous
15. A *nocturnal* march — 1. military 2. tragic 3. stirring 4. night 5. funereal
16. The *saturnine* doctor — 1. comforting 2. trustworthy 3. rambling 4. gloomy 5. skilled
17. To view with *equanimity* — 1. alarm 2. approbation 3. misgiving 4. calmness 5. misunderstanding
18. *Insouciance* of colleagues — 1. optimism 2. warning 3. indifference 4. attitudes 5. helpfulness
19. *Myriad* uses of wood — 1. constructive 2. common 3. particular 4. questionable 5. numberless
20. An *ineffable* quality — 1. indescribable 2. manly 3. measurable 4. transparent 5. desirable
21. A *whimsical* taxi driver — 1. odd 2. reckless 3. talkative 4. stolid 5. experienced
22. The science of *ornithology* — 1. trees 2. living 3. insects 4. flowers 5. birds
23. *Fecund* plant life — 1. fecund 2. prolific 3. decaying 4. aquatic 5. tropical
24. An *invidious* comparison — 1. truthful 2. offensive 3. clever 4. silly 5. favorable
25. Carefully *effaced* inscriptions — 1. copied 2. written 3. erased 4. preserved 5. transferred
26. A *fortuitous* resemblance — 1. family 2. natural 3. faint 4. close 5. chance
27. An *arch* foe — 1. foreign 2. cunning 3. arrogant 4. enervated 5. insignificant
28. A *saline* solution — 1. logical 2. salty 3. satisfactory 4. medical 5. mathematical
29. To participate in *chicanery* — 1. debate 2. frivolity 3. athletics 4. deception 5. ceremony
30. An *evanescent* thought — 1. fleeting 2. pragmatic 3. farcical 4. reverent 5. philosophical
31. A *droll* expression — 1. simple 2. trite 3. comforting 4. amusing 5. indignant
32. Men given *kudos* — 1. scholarships 2. recognition 3. commissions 4. honors 5. sentences
33. To establish *rapport* — 1. contact 2. policies 3. understanding 4. credit 5. bases
34. To give *succor* — 1. relief 2. assurance 3. awards 4. satisfaction 5. suggestions
35. An African *safari* — 1. emperor 2. expedition 3. aborigine 4. native 5. zebra
36. *Furtive* glances — 1. bold 2. loving 3. respected 4. sly 5. habitual
37. A *sardonic* look — 1. triumphant 2. wan 3. immaculate 4. weary 5. scornful
38. He spoke *fatuously* — 1. tirelessly 2. impartially 3. sensibly 4. moodily 5. foolishly
39. A *phlegmatic* disposition — 1. sanguine 2. dejected 3. calm 4. violent 5. troublesome
40. *Dilatory* behavior — 1. dogmatic 2. puerile 3. wise 4. delaying 5. kindly
41. *Exigent* problems — 1. omnipresent 2. critical 3. extra 4. domestic 5. confusing
42. A *chimerical* undertaking — 1. expensive 2. complicated 3. unnecessary 4. dramatic 5. visionary
43. A *paragon* of patience — 1. model 2. quality 3. lack 4. surfeit 5. reward
44. Incredibly *gauche* — 1. impolite 2. powerful 3. awkward 4. intelligent 5. haughty
45. To *avert* a strike — 1. arbitrate 2. end 3. prevent 4. foment 5. initiate
46. A *rubicund* man — 1. ruddy 2. fat 3. gluttonous 4. elfish 5. rational
47. To eye *truculently* — 1. slyly 2. endearingly 3. obtusely 4. fiercely 5. earnestly
48. A *tacit* admission — 1. boastful 2. sworn 3. guarded 4. unspoken 5. foolish
49. The *temerity* of youth — 1. skillfulness 2. pessimism 3. optimism 4. genius 5. rashness
50. *Fulsome* praise — 1. unusual 2. fanatic 3. insincere 4. unexpected 5. endless

Reprinted by permission. From Vocabulary Quiz, copyright 1957 by
G. & C. Merriam Co., Publishers of the Merriam-Webster Dictionaries.

Words	Prefix	Common Meaning	Root	Common Meaning
PRECEPT	pre-	(before)	capere	(take, seize)
DETAIN	de-	(away, from)	tenere	(hold, have)
INTERMITTENT	inter-	(between)	mittere	(send)
OFFER	ob-	(against)	ferre	(bear, carry)
INSIST	in-	(into)	stare	(stand)
MONOGRAPH	mono-	(alone, one)	graphein	(write)
EPILOGUE	epi-	(upon)	legein	(say, study of)
ASPECT	ad-	(to, towards)	specere	(see)
UNCOMPLICATED	un- com-	(not) (together with)	plicare	(fold)
NONEXTENDED	non- ex-	(not) (out of)	tendere	(stretch)
REPRODUCTION	re- pro-	(back, again) (forward)	ducere	(lead)
INDISPOSED	in- dis-	(not) (apart from)	ponere	(put, place)
OVERSUFFICIENT	over- sub-	(above) (under)	facere	(make, do)
MISTRANSCRIBE	mis- trans-	(wrong) (across, beyond)	scribere	(write)

FIGURE 8—1

Fourteen Master Words: Key to the Meanings
of Over 14,000 Words

Compiled by James I. Brown and reprinted by permission from Word
Study, copyright 1949 by G. & C. Merriam Co., Publishers of the
Merriam-Webster Dictionaries.

USING THE FOURTEEN MASTER WORDS

It has been estimated that 60 per cent of the English words in common use are made up partly or entirely of prefixes or roots derived from Latin and Greek. To find out which prefixes and roots of Latin and Greek origin appear most frequently in English words, Professor James I. Brown, of the University of Minnesota, recorded the number of times certain word-elements appeared in an unabridged dictionary. He found that 20 prefixes and 14 roots were parts of 14,000 relatively common English words, and of an estimated 100,000 words in that dictionary. He then compiled a list of common English words which contained the 20 prefixes and 14 roots among them. These words he called the *Fourteen Master Words*.[4] (See Figure 8–1.)

The value of this list is that it illustrates the way much of our language is constructed. If learned, it can help you recognize and understand many words without resorting to a dictionary. With one well-understood root word as the center, an entire "constellation" of words can be built up. Figure 8–2 shows such a constellation, based on the root "duct," from the Latin *ducere* (to lead). You will notice that it makes use of some of the twenty most common prefixes (see Figure 8–1) and of other prefixes and combining words as well as various suffixes or word endings. It does not exhaust all the possibilities, either; you should be able to think of several other words growing out of "duct."

[4] Professor Brown's findings are described in detail in the article "Reading and Vocabulary: 14 Master Words," which appeared in the May, 1949, issue of *Word Study,* published by G. & C. Merriam Co., Springfield, Mass.

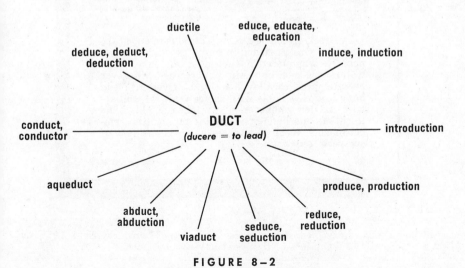

FIGURE 8–2

A Constellation of Words from One Root

LEARNING THE ORIGINS OF WORDS

Delving into word origins can be a pleasurable way of developing both your awareness and your understanding of words. Words take on more meaning and become more memorable when their "life stories" are unfolded.

Back of almost every word in the English language there is a "life story" that will come to many as a fascinating revelation. Our words have come to us from a multitude of sources. Some of them have lived for thousands of years and have played their parts in many lands and many civilizations. They may record ancient superstitions. They may be monuments to customs dating back to classical antiquity. They may reveal our ancestors' manners and beliefs, shrouded in the mists of ancient history. Words that you use today may have been the slang of Roman soldiers twenty centuries ago or the lingo of Malay savages. They may have been used by an Athenian poet or by an Anglo-Saxon farmer.[5]

The following is an example of how memorable a word can be when its origin is learned and can be vividly pictured:[6]

TANTALIZE

to torment with the punishment of Tantalus

In Greek mythology, King Tantalus offended the gods and was punished in an extraordinary manner. He was placed in the midst of a lake whose waters reached his chin but receded whenever he attempted to allay his thirst. Over his head hung branches laden with choice fruit, which likewise receded whenever he stretched out his hand to satisfy his hunger. Tantalus became the symbol of such teasing, and his name is the root of our verb *tantalize*.

[5] By permission, from *Interesting Origins of English Words*, copyright 1959 by G. & C. Merriam Co., Publishers of the Merriam-Webster Dictionaries.
[6] By permission, from *Picturesque Word Origins*, copyright 1933 by G. & C. Merriam Co., Publishers of the Merriam-Webster Dictionaries.

BEING DICTIONARY—MINDED

Every college student should own a good desk dictionary for ready reference. Especially recommended are *Webster's New Collegiate Dictionary* (Springfield, Mass.: G. & C. Merriam Co.); *The American College Dictionary* (New York: Random House); and *Webster's New World Dictionary of the American Language* (Cleveland: World Publishing Company). Keep your dictionary within arm's reach as you study, and develop the habit of consulting it.

For intensive word study there is no substitute for an unabridged dictionary. Locate the unabridged dictionaries in the library — normally you will find them in the reference room — and use them to supplement your own abridged desk dictionary. An unabridged dictionary gives more definitions, more about the derivation of words, more on usage. Good one-volume unabridged works include *Webster's New International Dictionary of the English Language* (G. & C. Merriam Co.), in either the second or third editions; and the *New Standard Dictionary of the English Language* (New York: Funk and Wagnalls). *The Oxford English Dictionary* or "OED" (Oxford, England: Clarendon Press), in 10 volumes and supplement, is indispensable for the historical study of words, but more detailed than you will need for most purposes.

The reference librarian can also help you find specialized dictionaries in various subjects which list technical terms not always found even in unabridged dictionaries. For such terms, however, your textbooks are the best sources for definitions.

USING VOCABULARY CARDS

The vocabulary card method is an effective technique for word study. For this you will need a supply of 3×5-inch index cards. When you come across an unfamiliar word, or a familiar one in unfamiliar use, write it on a card. An excellent plan is to write the sentence or phrase in which it occurs (underlining the word) to provide a meaningful context. Now look the word up in the dictionary and write it in syllables, with accent marks, and with pronunciation indicated if necessary. On the reverse side of the card, take down the definition which is most appropriate in the context. (For a technical term write the definition given in your textbook; special terms are usually defined when first introduced or else in a glossary.) If you want to pursue your study of a word in more detail, record also on the reverse side of the card any information you find about its derivation; for this information you may need to consult an unabridged dictionary and to look up several related words. Add secondary definitions if you wish. (Figure 8–3.)

Study your cards in this way: pronounce the word correctly; try to recall the definition without looking at it; then turn the card over to check your

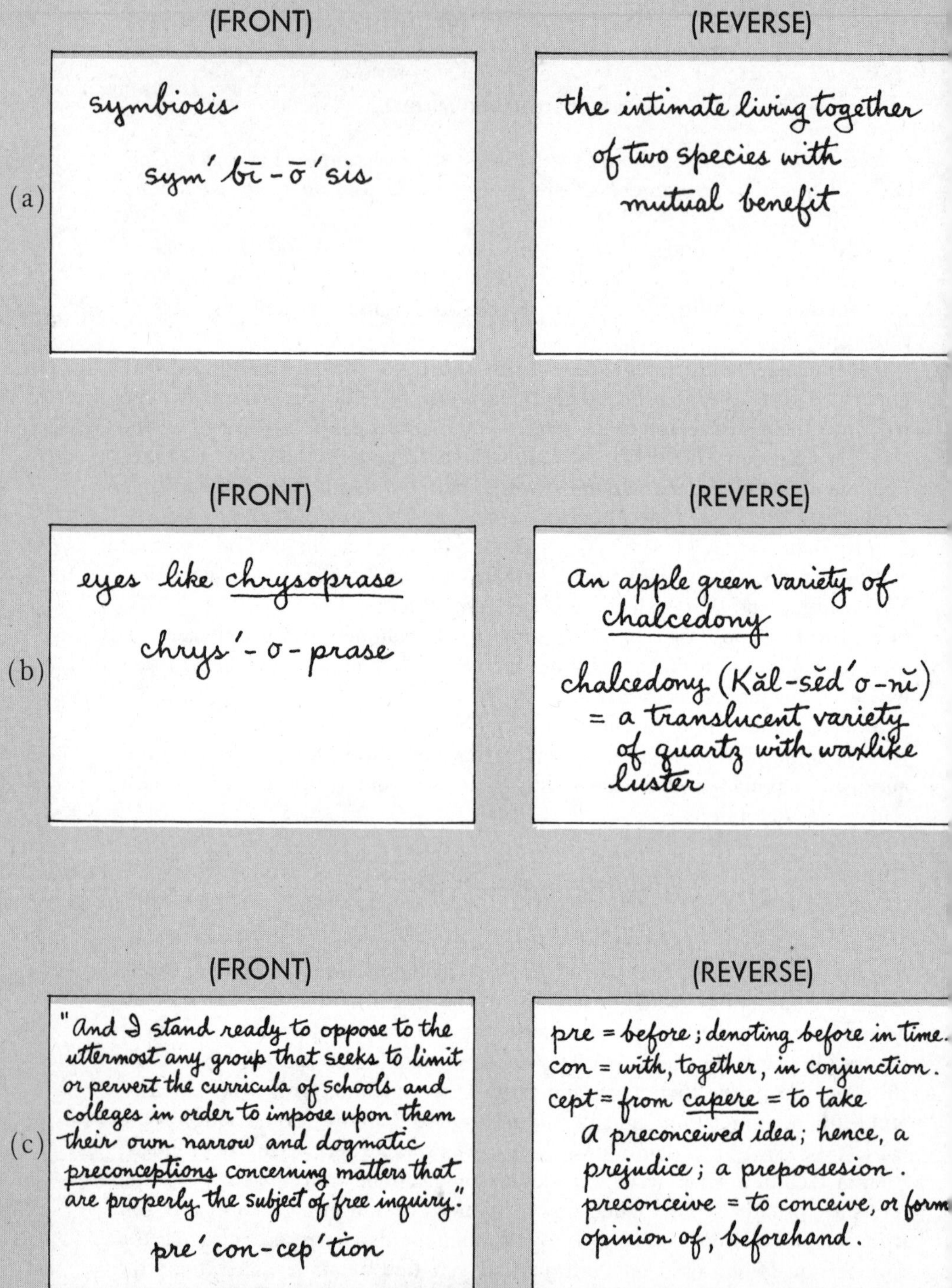

(a)

(FRONT)

symbiosis

sym' bī – ō' sis

(REVERSE)

the intimate living together
of two species with
mutual benefit

(b)

(FRONT)

eyes like chrysoprase

chrys'- o - prase

(REVERSE)

An apple green variety of
chalcedony

chalcedony (Kăl-sĕd'o-nĭ)
= a translucent variety
of quartz with waxlike
luster

(c)

(FRONT)

"And I stand ready to oppose to the
uttermost any group that seeks to limit
or pervert the curricula of schools and
colleges in order to impose upon them
their own narrow and dogmatic
preconceptions concerning matters that
are properly the subject of free inquiry."

pre' con-cep' tion

(REVERSE)

pre = before; denoting before in time.
con = with, together, in conjunction.
cept = from capere = to take
   A preconceived idea; hence, a
   prejudice; a prepossesion.
preconceive = to conceive, or form
   opinion of, beforehand.

FIGURE 8–3

Vocabulary Cards

*Vocabulary cards in varying degrees of detail: (a) a "key idea"
term defined from the textbook; (b) a word in a meaningful phrase
with secondary definition given; (c) a word in full sentence context,
with information on parts and derivation, and with a secondary
definition.*

recall. If you fail, place a dot in the upper right-hand corner, on the front of the card. The next time you go through your cards, a dot will remind you that you missed on a previous try. When a card has three or more dots, it is time to give that word some special attention.

The advantage of 3 × 5-inch cards is that they are convenient to carry about for study at odd moments. Recently a business executive told me he learned this system at Yale many years ago and has practiced it ever since. From his pocket he pulled some cards to emphasize his point: "I study a card or two every time I walk between the parking lot and the office."

Have a few blank cards with you at all times on which to record unfamiliar or particularly interesting words. Learning words which have puzzled or intrigued you will be immeasurably more valuable than memorizing a list made up for you by someone else.

ANSWERS to vocabulary quiz (page 59): 1 (2); 2 (1); 3 (4); 4 (4); 5 (1); 6 (3); 7 (5); 8 (5); 9 (1); 10 (3); 11 (3); 12 (1); 13 (2); 14 (5); 15 (4); 16 (4); 17 (4); 18 (3); 19 (5); 20 (1); 21 (1); 22 (5); 23 (2); 24 (2); 25 (3); 26 (5); 27 (2); 28 (2); 29 (4); 30 (1); 31 (4); 32 (4); 33 (3); 34 (1); 35 (2); 36 (4); 37 (5); 38 (5); 39 (3); 40 (4); 41 (2); 42 (5); 43 (1); 44 (3); 45 (3); 46 (1); 47 (4); 48 (4); 49 (5); 50 (3).

9

Concentration

A noted psychiatrist has said that people concentrate all the time during their waking hours. The trouble is that much of the time they concentrate on something other than the job in hand. Judging by the numbers who come to me for help, concentration is probably the major problem confronting college students.

Trouble in concentrating may come from many causes, often interrelated. For example, many students are so afraid of failing that the dread spectre of failure takes more of their attention than their study assignments. Anxiety causes them to do poor work, and this in turn intensifies the fear they started with. Some students never get off this treadmill. But many do; and nearly all can, if shown the way. It is encouraging that victory over one cause of failure often leads to victory over the entire complex.

Fortunately, the ability to concentrate can be improved by learning to recognize the causes of poor concentration, by learning to control these causes, and then by making this control habitual. The causes can be external or internal distractions, physical or mental fatigue, or lack of interest in the work to be done. All these, once recognized, can be overcome.

EXTERNAL DISTRACTION

College libraries, dormitories, fraternity and sorority houses are full of external distractions, ranging from blue eyes to banging doors; but these can be minimized if you will follow these suggestions:

1. Every student should have a desk which is used for studying and for no other purpose. In this way, he will build up a strong association of desk with active study. A desk used just for study is a place where books and papers may be left open so that the next study session is set up for a quick beginning.

2. In placing your desk in a room, or in choosing a chair in the library, make sure you face in the direction of fewest distractions. The desk should be outfitted for work. There should be paper and pencils at your fingertips, and textbooks, a dictionary, and other reference books within easy reach. Having your books and materials right at hand makes for efficiency.

3. For each subject studied, clear the desk to allow the maximum space for the papers and books you will need to use. Keep no pictures or ornaments on your desk to compete for your attention.

4. Study where you will hear as little noise as possible. If some noise is inescapable, train yourself to shut it out mentally. This, of course, takes extra effort. In college, studying to the tune of a radio or phonograph may be disastrous. Many students argue that they did it in high school and got good grades, even a scholarship. These students fail to realize that while routine work can be done to music, mastering new principles and masses of fact demands full concentration, and this is impossible while half the mind is booing a commercial or tapping out a tune. The high school student who studies against perpetual noise may get along, but he does so in spite of the distraction, not because of it.

5. If your dormitory or house is too noisy for effective study, then you *must* go to the library where you will find more suitable conditions. Nothing is more frustrating and wasteful than going over the same paragraph again and again because there is too much noise for you to absorb what you are reading. Noise within living quarters is one of the most serious single obstacles to effective study. Many students rationalize that it takes too much time to get to the library, and continue to put up with frustrations and annoyances. If they but knew it, two or three hours of efficient study in quiet surroundings does more good than ten hours in near bedlam. Many students find the walk to the library refreshing, and report that they can concentrate on their studies and actually get something done as they walk back and forth. I cannot stress the point too strongly: *Make the decision to find a quiet place to study in, and stick to it.*

6. Particularly in a library or a study hall, learn to avoid looking up from your work every time someone walks by. Nine out of ten students will look up, and it is easy to spend half one's time doing so. Permitting small distractions becomes a time-consuming habit. Think about this: raising your eyes from your work, whether or not you recognize the passer-by, results in much the same action. If you know him, you may nod or smile; if not, you may simply stare. But in neither case will you shout or slap him on the back, or (presumably) talk for an hour. So nothing is gained by looking up, but your train of thought is derailed and valuable time is lost forever.

INTERNAL DISTRACTIONS

To avoid internal distractions, the following suggestions are of proven value:

1. Don't go through an elaborate ritual of rearranging books, sharpening pencils, and getting a "last" snack before settling down to study. It helps many students to have a designated time to begin. They may say to themselves, "I will relax for half an hour after dinner and begin to study at 7:30." Unless they set a definite time to start, many students continue to put it

off indefinitely, on the theory that "a few more minutes won't hurt." Remember, the sooner you start, the sooner you will be free to do other things.

2. Many internal distractions can be avoided simply by scheduling one's time. Scheduling will help to eliminate conflict and the needless worry that goes into making frequent decisions on what and where to study. Scheduling is so important to good study habits that an entire chapter has been devoted to it (Chapter 2).

3. One of the worst time-wasters is daydreaming. Daydreaming is a way of escaping from hard work. Pleasant as it often is, it can become a vicious habit and must be combatted by the knowledge that it never got anybody any of the things he really wanted. If you recognize that it is a poor substitute for the real thing, and hark back to the job, you will be able to overcome the negative habit of daydreaming and to establish the positive habit of plunging directly and efficiently into your work. *This* is a habit which will stand you in good stead all your life.

4. Personal problems take an immense toll in time and emotion. This important subject is discussed in detail in Chapter 17.

5. If you are bothered by a poor grade or are having trouble with a particular subject, make an appointment with the instructor and talk the matter over. Most instructors are sympathetic and feel gratified when you come to them for help.

6. Set up realistic goals for study. If a student has hardly been studying at all, it is not realistic for him to announce suddenly: "Tonight I plan to study for six hours." The chances are that so much sustained effort will be too great for him, and he will only experience another discouraging failure. It is hard to make a radical change in one's habits all at once. To succeed, the change must be gradual. If that same student were to declare instead that he would study for two hours that first evening, he would have a far better chance of achieving his goal. And his success would encourage him to attempt increasingly longer periods of concentration. Success snowballs just as powerfully as failure.

7. To avoid worrying about the possibility of missing personal appointments, write down the times and events in chronological order. Keep this reminder where you will be sure to see it regularly. A desk calendar is ideal for the purpose. Having made a written reminder, you need no longer hold in mind appointments which have been a source of distraction.

PHYSICAL FATIGUE

Health directly affects the ability to study. It is hard to concentrate when hungry, sleepy, or run-down. Here are some suggestions for keeping in good physical condition.

1. Eat three regular meals a day, and get to sleep at a reasonable hour. Make eating and sleeping so habitual that they are no longer fair game for decisions. When habit takes over, you save your thinking power for your studies.

2. Another common cause of fatigue is poor study conditions. Unnecessary physical strain can be avoided by following these suggestions:

(*a*) Use a good straight-backed chair, so that you can sit in an alert position while studying. The chair should not be conducive to drowsiness or daydreaming, and should be of a comfortable height.

(*b*) Study in a good light. For study, lighting engineers recommend a low diffused light throughout the room plus local or functional lighting for books and papers, ordinarily provided by an adjustable lamp close to the user. The intensity of the local light will depend to some extent on the individual. If you have a standard incandescent lamp, try bulbs of different strengths to find which is best for you. (I personally like a two-bulb fluorescent lamp with positioning arms, the kind which draftsmen use.) The fatigue-producing factors in lighting are two: insufficient light, and glare from such surfaces as desk tops and papers. To cut down glare, use a desk blotter and experiment with the position of your lamp.

(*c*) Be sure the room is well ventilated. It is better to have it on the cool side. Put on a sweater if it is too cool. Many students find it helpful to have a thermometer in their room.

3. Include in your schedule enough time for recreation and exercise. The student who does not tends to drag out his study hours wastefully.

4. Many students find sleepiness one of their greatest problems. Sleepiness can result from real fatigue or from a subconscious desire to avoid dull or unpleasant tasks. One way to fight sleepiness is to take frequent five-minute breaks. Another is to pace the floor slowly while reading a book or reciting a lesson aloud. Still another is to schedule recreation or academic assignments involving physical activity (such as sorting cards or rearranging notes) at hours when you ordinarily find it hard to study. Psychologists find that each person's sleepy period occurs at about the same time every day or evening. One word of warning: too many students rationalize that it is better to give in to the urge to sleep and that when they wake up they will be refreshed. Few students report this happy result. Rather, they awake to a formidable pile of work undone. It is far better to combat the desire to sleep, get the work done, and then go to bed at the usual time with a clear conscience.

MENTAL FATIGUE

Research has shown that it is all but impossible to develop mental fatigue by studying. We get "tired" readily enough, but this happens because we are bored with the subject, not because bodily wastes accumulate in muscles and brain. Push away a book on physics with the comment "I'm exhausted," then pick up a newspaper or a magazine, and you may find yourself reading avidly, without signs of fatigue, for an hour or so.

Fatigue is related to motivation as well as to interest. The American philosopher and psychologist William James, with his usual insight, knew this half a century ago. He wrote:

Everyone knows what it is to start a piece of work, either intellectual or muscular, feeling stale. . . . And everybody knows what it is to "warm up" to his job. The process of warming up gets particularly striking in the phenomenon known as "second wind." On usual occasions we make a practice of stopping an occupation as soon as we meet the first effective layer (so to call it) of fatigue. We have then walked, played, worked "enough," so we desist. That amount of fatigue is an efficacious obstruction on this side of which our usual life is cast. But if an unusual necessity forces us to press onward, a surprising thing occurs. The fatigue gets worse up to a certain critical point, when gradually or suddenly it passes away, and we are fresher than before. We have evidently tapped a level of new energy masked until then by the fatigue-obstacle usually obeyed. There may be layer after layer of this experience. A third and a fourth "wind" may supervene. Mental activity shows the phenomenon as well as physical, and in exceptional cases we may find, beyond the very extremity of fatigue-distress, amounts of ease and power that we never dreamed ourselves to own, — sources of strength habitually not taxed at all, because habitually we never push through the obstruction, never pass those early critical points.

For many years I have mused on the phenomenon of second wind, trying to find a physiological theory. It is evident that our organism has stored-up reserves of energy that are ordinarily not called upon, but that may be called upon: deeper and deeper strata of combustible or explosible material, discontinuously arranged, but ready for use by anyone who probes so deep, and repairing themselves by rest as well as do the superficial strata. Most of us continue living unnecessarily near our surface. . . .[1]

CREATING INTEREST

Most students find it particularly hard to concentrate on "boring" or "difficult" subjects. The difficult subject is often the one the student is not interested in and so does not care to read and think about. Frequently the subject remains "boring" and "difficult" simply because his knowledge remains meager. Worse still, it pulls down his marks and upsets his composure and self-confidence. Students who venture past the alien frontier are almost always pleasantly surprised. No intelligent mind, reading and thinking about any subject, can long fail to find in it something of interest and value.

Following the six suggestions below will both help in overcoming boredom and shed light on the technique of gaining a true education.

1. Adopt an active mental attitude. It is not enough simply to *read* the assigned number of pages in a textbook; the object should be to *understand* them.

2. Reading can be made active if you convert the author's concepts into

[1] William James, "The Energies of Men," in *Memories and Studies* (New York: Longmans, Green, and Co., 1911), pp. 229–231. Copyright, 1911, by Henry James, Jr. Reprinted by permission of Paul R. Reynolds & Son, 599 Fifth Avenue, New York 17, N.Y.

opposites and then ask why these opposites are not true. This mental exercise makes the material so familiar that remembering it is no problem. Best of all, you will be mentally alert.

3. Create an interest by saying to yourself, "I'll try to master this bit."

4. To gain strength in independent thinking and judgment, first grasp the main point and the steps in the discussion. Then, when you meet such words as, "from the above it logically follows that . . ." stop reading and try to anticipate the conclusion. Write it out or say it aloud; then compare your version with the author's. Where yours differs, try to determine how and why. If you sincerely want to get the most from your time and effort in reading an assignment, this technique should keep you awake and alert. Better still, you will not only acquire facts; you will learn to think better and you will grow in wisdom.

5. Interest in a subject can be cultivated by starting with very elementary books about it. Far from wasting your time, such books can help you to understand basic principles which more advanced books take for granted. They can thus give you a firm foundation to build on.

6. Another way to arouse interest in a "dull" subject is through reading and experiment. Reading about the excitement which accompanied the discovery of radium may stimulate an interest in chemistry; a trip to the botanical garden or to a greenhouse may jog a flagging interest in botany more effectively than a dozen textbooks.

10

Remembering What You Learn

A person with a perfect memory would retain for life every fact and every concept he learned. Nobody does this, and it is just as well. Our minds would be cluttered with oddments from grocery lists, telephone books, and newspaper stories, and we would hold onto unpleasant experiences as tenaciously as we retain pleasant ones.

Since forgetting plays such an important part in academic life, we should try to understand what causes it. Many psychologists explain forgetting by the theory of "interference" or "retroactive inhibition." In this view, new learning gets in the way of the recall of earlier learning. For example, if a student learns the dates of twenty major battles, and then the dates of ten minor ones, he may have difficulty recalling the first twenty dates because of interference from the ten learned later. The more the intervening material resembles the original, and the more closely the later learning follows upon the earlier, the greater seems the likelihood of interference.

MNEMONIC DEVICES

Whatever the cause of it, forgetting is the bane of students. To combat it, many invent (or inherit) *mnemonic devices* — words, sentences, rhymes, and other formulas which associate a complex principle or body of fact with a simple statement that is easy to remember. A classic example is the old jingle, "Thirty days hath September," by which most of us learned the irregularities of our calendar. Another is the spelling rule:

i before *e* except after *c*
or when pronounced *a*
as in *neighbor* and *weigh*.

Still another is this device for remembering the value of π, the ratio of the circumference of a circle to its diameter (3.1415926535895+), a rhyme in which the key is the number of letters in each word:

```
3   1   4   1   5       9
```
How I wish I could determine
```
2   6   5
```
Of circle round
```
3   5   8
```
The exact relation
```
9       5
```
Arkimedes found.

But except for purely mechanical matters like the number of days in the months or the value of π, mnemonic systems are of doubtful utility. Their chief fault is that they side-step the intrinsic meaning of the material being learned. It then remains a compartmentalized parcel of data which is mechanically taken out of the mnemonic context only when needed. The student may learn a sequence of names and dates this way, but the chances are he does not learn much about them. If, on the other hand, he learns the same list directly and meaningfully, he can integrate it into his general knowledge for use in relation to other facts and ideas.

An example of how mnemonic systems break down came to light in one of my lectures. A graduate student said he remembered the twelve cranial nerves by the initial letters in the following rhyme:

> On old Olympus' topmost top
> A fat armed German viewed a hop.

When I asked him to name the nerves, he confessed that he had forgotten them![1]

Artificial mnemonic systems have two additional faults. The slightest error in the jingle or anagram can throw you off completely. And the time spent in memorizing it is rarely justified by the result.

Students generally use mnemonic devices in preparing for examinations, often in desperation, hoping somehow to "get by." But facts so learned — if they really *are* learned — are usually retained for a relatively short time. Students who resort to cramming in this fashion, realizing that they are gearing for an examination only, often promise themselves that afterwards, when they mistakenly think they will have more time, they will re-study the material and "really learn" it. Such re-studying is rare, since the student who crams for examinations is usually the one who never has time to do what must be done, let alone tasks which require extra time.

In spite of the welter of claims for a variety of memory systems, there seem to be only three things necessary for good memory — and by this I mean memory which persists for any length of time. These three things are: attitude; a knowledge of the relationships between the memorized material and other material; and review.

[1] Incidentally, the nerves are: the olfactory, optic, oculomotor, trochlear, trigeminal, abducens, facial, auditory, glossopharyngeal, vagus, accessory, and hypoglossal.

ATTITUDE

In results, there is all the difference in the world between a positive and a negative attitude. Given two students of equal intelligence and background, the one who approaches an assignment or a lecture with the will to learn and remember will do vastly better than the one who merely does what he must to salve his conscience or fulfill an unpleasant duty. The first reads and listens actively; and in the attempt to fit new facts and concepts into the framework of what he already knows, he tends to understand accurately and remember clearly. The other reads and listens passively, content with going through the motions, forming hazy impressions certain of faulty recall — trusting to luck that what he reads and hears will somehow come forth when he needs it.

Many students have asked me, "Does everyone have a mental attitude about everything?" And I answer, "Certainly. We all have a predisposition or 'bias' to act in one way rather than another, even though several avenues of approach are open to us. For some reason, we pick one approach over other plausible ones." A student who goes to a lecture mentally set to be bored will find little in the lecture. If he sits down at his study desk "just to look things over casually," he will arise from the study desk with only casual impressions.

If your bias is toward learning a subject or solving a problem, you have already won half the battle. You'll remember what you want to remember. The student who "can't" remember mathematical equations is often able to recite the batting averages of dozens of baseball players. The student who finds physics "too complex" may be able to discuss the complexities of his automobile with eloquence.

But, you ask, aren't some subjects *really* dull? Dullness is not inherent in any subject, though every subject is dull to some people. It is dull to those who have neither interest nor motivation and whose attitude is indifferent or hostile. How does one get around this difficulty? In general, the more we know about anything, the more interest we have in it. Outside reading is one way to break the ice. Reading biographies of famous chemists — feeling the excitement they felt in their discoveries — can make "dull" chemistry come alive. Reading about famous battles or how the pyramids were built can create an interest in history, strategy, engineering, or human rights.

Another way to stimulate interest is to ask other students how they feel about a subject. Ask an engineering student, for example, why he gets pleasure in working a set of problems and you may see that to him they represent not mental torture but human situations. Explore the motives and interests of other students. Talk, talk, and talk about your subjects. This is learning — a good discussion of a controversial lecture may be worth hours of study.

A third way to stimulate interest is to go to the subject's native ground. Get a feeling for botany, for example, by examining the parts of a flower in a field — not just by memorizing facts in textbooks. Learn what psychology is about by visiting a clinic or a mental hospital. Nothing shows you so quickly what a subject is for, and why it is worth studying, as seeing how it applies to human problems and human affairs.

THE IMPORTANCE OF RELATING FACTS

New facts can be remembered more easily when you fit them into a framework as you learn them. This framework can be built by preliminary skimming of the material before settling down to learning it.

For example, when studying a poem, it is best to read and re-read it in its entirety until you have a feeling for its organization and some grasp of its main idea. Then, if you memorize portions of the poem, you can keep in mind the relationship of the parts to the whole. Similarly, when studying history, it is best to place events in relation to the broader picture — the entire era — before attempting to analyze them in detail.

THE PSYCHOLOGY OF REVIEWING: IMMEDIATE RECALL

Effective review, the third technique for reinforcing memory, involves a good deal more than passively "looking over" notes and reading. It involves the *active* technique of mastering assignments by effective methods. Most forgetting takes place immediately after initial learning. In one psychological study,[2] five groups of students were tested at different time intervals to discover how much of a psychology lecture they remembered. The results follow:

Group	Time Interval	Amount Remembered
I	none	62 per cent
II	$\frac{1}{2}$ week	50 per cent
III	1 week	37 per cent
IV	2 weeks	30 per cent
V	8 weeks	23 per cent

One of the best ways to retain information is by *immediate recall*. This means actively discussing, reciting, or writing, in your own words, what you have just read or heard.

I have repeatedly demonstrated the value of immediate recall by showing a reading film at a fairly fast rate to two groups of students. Group I is then asked to go over the material mentally for one minute before resuming regular class work. Group II resumes class work at once, without mental review. After a week, both groups are asked to answer ten questions on the film. The average grade for Group I is 85 per cent; for Group II, 45 per

[2] Harold E. Jones, "Experimental Studies of College Teaching," *Archives of Psychology*, 10 (1923), 30.

cent. *One minute spent in immediate recall nearly doubles retention.* Immediate recall is the only way to hammer new knowledge into clear and correct impressions before forgetting takes its heavy toll.

SOME FURTHER SUGGESTIONS

Here are four additional suggestions for improving your retention:

1. Get correct first impressions. Ideas, facts, and relationships learned incorrectly or superficially will remain faulty and imprecise unless later revised. And it is hard to change a mistaken first impression. You can save a great deal of time if you make the effort to get things right the first time.

2. Study subjects in a sequence which will hold to a minimum the interference from subsequent learning. Since interference appears to be strongest when the later learning closely resembles and closely follows the earlier, try to space out your study for courses with similar subject matter. Thus it would be better to follow an hour's study of French with an hour of history or chemistry rather than of Spanish.

3. Overlearn; that is, study a subject *beyond* the time required for the first perfect recall. Overlearning is one of the most effective ways to insure remembering.

4. Finally, as we saw in Chapter 3, it will aid the memory to understand the pattern or organization of material, to group facts and ideas meaningfully, being alert to notice similarities and differences.

11

Examinations

Examinations, like death and taxes, are inevitable. The wise student takes them in stride and makes them work for him. Besides allowing the instructor to check on student progress, exams permit the student to check on his own progress. Studying for an examination should be regarded as an important part of learning; it gives an opportunity to pull one's knowledge together, reflect on main points, and gain the new insights that can be the most exciting part of any course.

Examinations should be approached seriously but without undue worry. Grades on exams may mean the difference between passing and failing. On the other hand, it is dangerous to become panicky; you then tend to press too hard rather than to work methodically. Any athlete will tell you that pressing is a sure way to lose control. Fear limits perception, understanding, and general effectiveness, the very qualities you need most in an exam.

STUDYING FOR AN EXAMINATION

The first thing to learn is that no tricks or short cuts will help you if you don't know your subject. The surest way to do well on an exam is to keep up with your work and review your reading and lecture notes periodically. Studying for exams will then be no more than a final, thorough review that brings the material together. The best way to remove the fear of examinations is to know your subject through and through.

In reviewing for an examination, it is necessary to memorize and understand a considerable amount of factual data. But this is not enough. You must synthesize, find the organizing principles, and see interrelationships.

You may well ask at this point how to go about getting the whole picture. One way is first to go through your textbook chapters, your reading notes, and your lecture notes, and to pick out the main topics. Looking at these uncluttered by details and supporting material, you will be able to see the over-all development of ideas. Once you understand how ideas combine into a logical whole, you are ready to study details and supporting materials. These will be easier to remember because there will be main points around which they can be organized.

REFLECTING ON WHAT YOU HAVE LEARNED

Unless you reflect, memorized data will remain in a set, brittle state. Many a student has failed an exam because he thought that with the facts in mind he could play it by ear. Unfortunately, during an exam you have little time to reflect. You must think about the material, and make it flexible for your use, during your pre-examination study.

Reflecting on the material means examining the material from your own point of view, discovering implications that are not explicitly stated, perhaps questioning a thesis or a conclusion. When you can thus manipulate your facts and ideas, you are in control of them. To get practice, try playing with the material. See how the facts might be combined differently. Think up questions an instructor might ask. Even the act of formulating questions will help you, because you will be discriminating between the important ideas and the unimportant ones. Then answer each question by writing out the answer just as you would in the examination. (The best way to practice for anything is to duplicate the actual conditions as closely as possible.) In answering the questions you will be marshalling ideas and facts from different parts of the reading assignments and the lectures and will be arranging them in a different order from that in which you studied them. This is exactly what an examination seeks to make you do.

There is no substitute for this kind of studying. The student who spends his time thinking about gimmicks and short cuts would be far better off if he put that time into the kind of study suggested above.

KNOWING YOUR INSTRUCTOR

Another useful aid in studying for examinations is finding out what kinds of questions your instructor usually asks. This is not a matter of trying to outsmart him, but of harmonizing your approach with his. Some teachers emphasize relationships and synthesis; some are most interested in interpretations and applications; others stress knowledge of specific names, dates, events, definitions, and experiments. You can often get clues from the way the instructor lectures, the questions he asks in class, the assignments he gives. And for the first exam in a course, you are entitled to ask him what kind of questions to expect. For an objective test you will want to do a lot of memorizing of facts, names, dates, and figures. For an essay exam you will want to study general concepts and theories — but don't forget that specific names and facts must be given to support generalizations!

THE DANGERS OF CRAMMING

Crowding weeks of work into a few hours is no substitute for studying and reviewing, portion by portion, over a long period of time. If your goal in college is to gain knowledge — as it should be — cramming will not

The Hopi

A. Speech
1. Uto-Aztecan family (Ute, Paiute, Shoshone)

B. Subsistence – Economic Life
1. Skillful farmers — growing maize (mainstay), beans, squash,
2. Main fields not irrigated — small gardens irrigated. Cotton.
3. Domestic animals not important.
   a. turkeys — for feathers.
   b. sheep — for wool.
4. Wild flora — onions, potatoes, tobacco — yucca for soap.
5. Hunting
   a. rabbit

C. Settlement & Houses
1. Proximity of water
2. Desire for security — mesa residence.
3. Clay, Sandstone, mud — terraced effect — hole in top reached by ladder.
4. Only women own houses.
   a. matrilocal residence — brings together matrilineal kin.
   b. kinship groups are strong.

D. Crafts
1. Basketry (not too good).
2. Loom work — wool has become the principal textile material.
3. Pottery (coiled) painted.

E. Division of Labor
1. Men
   a. most of farming.
   b. spin, weave, tan skins, make clothing for selves & wives.
   c. housebuilding: both sexes work.
2. Women
   a. make pottery.
   b. tend gardens.

F. Trade
1. Other Pueblo
2. Paiute, Apache, Navaho.

G. Society – Lineage & Clan
1. Typical matrilocal residence. —— Underlie the clan system.
2. Houses owned by women. —— " " " "
3. All-important ceremonials associated with maternal lineage.
4. Clans are exogamous.
5. Clans have totemic names, but do not believe descended from totem.

H. Family & Clan
1. Boy accompanies father to cornfields; learns from him.

I. Government
1. Chief — head of Flute ceremony.
2. Power vested in hierarchical council of headmen.
3. Town chief must learn long ceremonial chants.

FIGURE 11–1

Studying for an Examination

Outline summary of lecture notes in sociology

help you. The facts learned hurriedly late at night will be forgotten as soon as the examination is over. If it is not a final exam, you will have to learn the material all over again later in the year; hence, in the long run, you actually save time by studying thoroughly as you go.

In addition, there is no guarantee that cramming will get you through. The pressure of time forces you to memorize facts out of context rather than to understand the concepts which the facts support. Disjointed, undigested facts are not much help in essay questions that require an understanding of principles and concepts.

Cramming is bad also for psychological reasons. The excessive tension and anxiety block the learning process. Then, too, the last-minute race against unpreparedness undermines your confidence and thereby lowers your mental alertness.

Don't forget, either, that by cramming for one subject you are upsetting your normal study schedule and falling behind in other courses. Cramming can thus become a vicious circle that leaves you no time for real learning.

THE NIGHT BEFORE

Some time, just before an important exam, someone is going to advise you to "relax and take in a movie." This advice has misled countless numbers of students — some who are all too ready to be persuaded away from their books, and others who honestly believe that they are doing a psychologically wise thing by taking in a movie the night before an exam.

The fact is, whether you are well prepared for the examination or not, you will be making a mistake to go to the movies just before it. If you are not prepared, a movie is not going to advance your preparation, and the underlying anxiety you feel will not permit you even the doubtful benefits of relaxation. The chances are that you will attempt to make up for lost time by working far into the night (*after* that "relaxing" movie) and will face the examination in the morning with a tired body and mind.

Even if you know the subject well and feel fully prepared, movies just before an examination are dangerous because *any* occupation involving your mind tends to interfere with previous learning. It is better to spend the evening in a quiet final review, go to bed early, and then face the examination the next morning mentally and physically awake.

"Relax and take in a movie — *after* the exam" is much better advice.

"ON YOUR MARK — GET SET!"

Some students are so tense and anxious to get going on an examination that they don't take time to "get set." A false start can be terribly costly. Hours of careful and conscientious preparation can be canceled out by a failure to note and follow directions, a careless reading of a question, or an unwise allocation of time.

Greek Race

Unity, well-rounded

The early Greeks were a vigorous people who constantly strove to achieve a well-rounded life — a unity of human knowledge. The Greeks did not have a departmental view. They believed that one man should know all things in one lifetime. The well-rounded Greek, in addition to being well versed in the arts, had to be an athlete, soldier, and statesman.

Competition

The Greeks loved competition. For example, they got together for athletic games each year. The athletic competitions best known to us were the games held at Mount Olympus and at Delphi.

Human-Image

A strong religious force permeated their lives. The early Greek religion was an interpretation of nature — polytheism. The Greeks invested the gods with a human image in order to define these forces as tangible beings. These gods had greater power than humans, but they possessed human frailties. There was a close connection between government and religion. Every city was supposed to have been established by some god. For example, Athena was supposed to have founded Athens and the people were descended from her.

Religion — concrete terms

Religion with the Greek was expressed in concrete terms. He sacrificed living animals to the gods and in that way established a contract. He gave the god the animal; therefore, the god should give the Greek what he desired. This concrete religion made the Greek feel at home in the world. The Greek further developed his religion to foretell the future. He used such devices as inspecting animal entrails and oracles. One of the most famous of the oracles was at Delphi which was used by the Athenians. Apollo was supposed to have dwelled there.

Death

Death was not looked upon as "eternal bliss." They called it "black death." They loved life because they lived fully and in the midst of it. The Greek citizen practically lived in the market place.

Government

No attempt was made to establish a federation. Never thought of central government. The Greek could not visualize a representative-type of government. It was the duty of every free-born citizen to speak his mind and to vote on all issues. He could not see one man representing a whole group. This individual freedom was a great asset toward the development of literature.

Slaves

The Greek was free to devote all his time in striving for perfection — toward becoming a well-rounded individual because the slaves did all the common work. This constant striving for perfection has resulted in their production of masterpieces in literature, sculpture, and architecture which we, in turn, have inherited.

FIGURE 11–2

Studying for an Examination

Paragraph-style summary of lecture notes in history

1. *Follow directions.* If you are asked to "Take either (*a*) or(*b*)," notice the *either-or* and don't defeat yourself by writing on both questions. If you are asked to "Write briefly on five of the following," don't ruin your chances by overlooking the directions and writing on only one.

2. *Read questions carefully.* Be sure you know exactly what they call for. If you are asked to contrast and compare two things, a description or résumé of each in turn — no matter how well done — is not a satisfactory answer. "Name," "Describe," "Explain," "Discuss," "Identify," "Compare," "Comment on," and similar directives mean different things and require different kinds of answers.

3. *Plan your time.* Usually the approximate amount of time that should be given to each question is indicated on the examination sheet. Follow this suggested allocation of time as closely as you can. If you spend 45 minutes on a question for which 15 minutes is allowed, you will doubtless achieve a more detailed answer than you otherwise would — but more detailed than is appropriate in the situation. Moreover, you will have short-changed yourself 30 minutes which you are going to need badly for other questions. The suggested time allocations are a clue to the importance or weight of the questions, and you should plan your answers with these times in mind. When no times are indicated, make an advance plan of your own. Look quickly over the exam to see how many questions there are and divide up the time to allow more for the "hard" questions and less for the "easy" ones. An examination calls on your ability to select as well as to display information; it tests your judgment as well as your knowledge.

ESSAY EXAMINATIONS

When you get the examination sheet, read all the questions through rapidly. Then you won't write information in one place when you could use it better in another. As you read, jot down beside each question any pertinent facts or ideas which occur to you. If choices are given, decide now which questions to answer. Note or estimate the time you have for each question. Remember, unanswered questions contribute no points.

Before starting to write, organize ideas and facts into some logical order. A brief outline will give structure to your answer and make it easier for you to concentrate fully on the question. There is nothing like a well-organized answer to convince the instructor of your control over the material. Be sure to note whether you are asked to discuss, describe, explain, compare, contrast, or the like. Don't think that giving an answer in a slightly different way than asked for will be just as good. On the other hand, if you can't write as directed, a slightly off-target answer is better than none.

Start on the easiest questions first. Getting down to work reduces anxiety. Your confidence rises when you complete a question or two, and your normal work habits take over.

A well-organized essay answer will be composed of the three following elements (see Figures 11-3 and 11-4):

1. *Thesis statement.* Start with a thesis sentence or paragraph. This will help you organize the rest of your answer.

2. *Supporting material.* Support your thesis statement by citing specific names, dates, and examples; noting exceptions; showing relationships; suggesting implications; establishing a time-frame where relevant; and ending with a summarizing sentence or paragraph.

3. *Transitional words and phrases.* Careful transitions will make your train of thought clear to the reader and show him how you are developing and relating your ideas and facts. For example, if you are adding another supporting fact to one you have already given, say, "In addition. . . ." If the added fact is equal in importance to the one already cited, say, "Equally important is. . . ." Lead the reader through your answer by giving him explicit directions such as these.

Leave space between answers. You may need it for ideas that occur to you after you have gone on to another question.

Be alert for questions which contain information or suggest ideas useful in answering other questions. But beware of the wily instructor who may thus be setting a trap!

You may run into questions that you consider unfair or think you can't answer. Don't waste energy reacting emotionally to them; you can't change them. It is best to leave such questions until the last; but don't leave them unanswered. Think the question through in relation to the course and to the facts you do know; then write the best answer you can. You can't lose anything by trying, and you may elicit from your instructor a valuable clue on why you are wrong.

Don't be the first one to leave the examination room. If you have time to spare, read over your paper. You may be able to raise your grade simply by inserting a missing word, rewriting a poor sentence, or correcting misspellings. Check your answers by asking yourself, "Is this a logical answer? a complete answer?" If it is not, you still have time to do something about it, in the extra space which you left between answers.

COMMON STUDENT ERRORS

When I asked one instructor about the most common errors students make in essay-type history examinations, he effectively summarized them as follows:

"Many students fail," he said, "to label historical movements. They do not state the 'time frame.' They give no idea whether the movement extended over decades or centuries. We don't insist on exact dates, but we do want to know what the 'time slice' is.

"Again, many students remain on the general level. I tell my students in class, 'Nail down generalities with examples.' Even after such a warning,

"name"
"indicate"

Places in context.
Thesis sentence.
Pre-outlines points.
Transitional
   sentence

Word analysis:
   gives specific
   examples

Interpretative
   reading: gives
   specific
   techniques

Purpose:
   How to do it

Structure:
   gives specific
   examples

Question: Name and briefly indicate several specific methods which
classroom teacher may employ to aid her students in improving the
reading skills. Consider this question in the context of the subject are
in which you plan to teach.

A student's answer: I plan to teach high school English. To aid m
students in improving their reading skills, I would teach them wor
analysis, how to read between the lines and interpret what they a
reading, how to read with a purpose — and for different purposes –
and how to better understand the structure of what they are readin
I shall discuss each of these methods briefly:

(A) Reading ability is greatly improved when the student has
grasp of most of the words with which he is dealing. In order
increase my students' working vocabulary I would teach them how
analyze words in context. We would learn prefixes, suffixes, and roo
and would learn how to analyze these and put them together. Wor
analysis would also involve figuring out words from their context
By practicing these skills, the students should be better able to hand
new words in their future reading.

(B) Interpretative reading or reading between the lines is anoth
means to the end of improved reading which I would teach. To he
students interpret what they read, I would have them read practic
passages — especially of poetry — and have them answer such que
tions as "What was the author's attitude toward Silas Marner, based o
her description of him?" or "What did the poet think of the girl abo
whom he wrote, 'Your face is like a rose.' ?"

(C) Reading with a purpose is basic to comprehension in ar
subject area. To get students used to reading with a purpose I wou
ask specific questions about the material, specifically relating to settin
character, etc. To get them used to reading for various purposes, I
introduce various material — magazines, novels, poems, etc.

(D) I would try to improve students' reading skills by teachir
them the structure of writings — the kinds of paragraphs, location
topic sentences, etc. Practice in writing, and exercise along this lir
would be beneficial.

FIGURE 11–3

A Well-Organized Answ

I receive papers without a specific, concrete name of a person, group, or geographical location.

"Some students, on the other hand, fill a booklet with facts, but never give the *why* of it all. What good are the facts if they don't know what the facts stand for?

"Though we warn students about illegible writing, we keep right on getting papers that are almost unreadable. This may be incidental, as far as knowledge is concerned, but it affects grades just the same. Yes, I try to understand a scribbled word here and there. I try to make out some words from context. But to ponder, decipher, and guess is not part of the job. If the student knows the answer, it is *his* job to write it so that I can read it. Scribbling is downright rude and inconsiderate.

"We want a well-organized essay. We urge the students to start with a thesis sentence. We suggest that they make a brief outline on the inside front cover of the test booklet as an aid to organizing their thoughts and to make the thesis sentence meaningful. But what do we get? A stream-of-consciousness answer.

"As I read some of the answers, I find myself muttering, 'What does the question *ask*? . . . Well, then, answer it!' I always suspect an answer which is off-focus. When a student doesn't know much about the question, he often slips to either side of it, into an area about which he knows a little bit more. Then he lays it on, thinking that a mountain of facts will obscure his shift off the topic.

"Actually, all a student needs to do is to know his subject cold, read the question carefully, make a slim outline, start off with a topic sentence, and then support it — and I mean *support* it. That's all there is to it."

STANDARDIZED TESTS

Standardized tests are not made up by your instructor or the department, but are available nationally and are usually characterized by separate answer sheets on which you write. Each standardized test item usually offers three or more alternate answers. Since each possible answer may be partly correct, study the question to be sure you know exactly what has been asked. Eliminate first the alternates with the least merit. Re-read the question and the remaining alternates, then select the best answer.

In a timed test, every second counts. Squeezing in two or three *more* right answers may mean the difference between a below-average grade and an above-average one. Here are some suggestions to help you save valuable minutes and channel your feeling of urgency into positive achievement:

1. Keep the test booklet and the answer sheet close together, so as not to subject the eye, hand, and head to unnecessarily long shifts from one to the other.

2. Place the answer sheet to the right of the booklet, instead of to the left. The disadvantage of having the answer sheet at the left is that the

"mean" — Answer should be interpretative

Question: What did Thorndike mean when he said, "Read- ing is a thinking process"?

Excellent thesis paragraph

A student's answer: When Thorndike said that reading i a thinking process he was disagreeing with the view tha many people hold that reading is a purely mechanica process, one in which the eye simply and passively register words and sends them to the brain. Thorndike was tryin to say that there is more to reading than this and tha reading is an active, rather than a passive procedure.

"amplify" — good transi- tional word

Underlined key words only

To amplify his statement, we see that reading as thinking process involves comprehension not simply per ception of the printed matter. The reader must involve hi "thinking cap" to determine the meaning of the words. H must ascribe particular meanings to the words, relate then to his own experience in order to give them real significanc to him, understand their relations to each other and under stand the ideas they form. He must use his power of reason ing in order to interpret what he reads.

"then" — indicates summary & end

In reading, then, the reader must actively ask himsel questions about the material and seek the answers to thes questions. He must read between the lines; he must extrac the main idea from each paragraph and must realize whic are the significant details. He must think about and be full aware of what he is reading while he is reading it! This i real comprehension — this is truly the reading proces structural knowledge and thought. He must be aware o what kind of a paragraph he is reading. Such awarenes is also necessary to this process.

FIGURE 11–4

A Well-Organized Answ

right arm must cross the booklet to mark the answer, thus covering the test so that it is hard to locate the next question quickly.

3. Avoid unnecessary retracing (blackening) of spaces on the answer sheet. One bold, deliberate mark is sufficient. On a 40-minute test, as much as 10 per cent of the total time can be wasted in retracing marks. Also, one deliberate mark will be easier to erase if necessary. Remember that if you wish to change an answer you must erase the original mark completely. If a residue of the original mark is present, in addition to another mark, the test item may be counted as incorrect by an electronic scoring machine.

4. If you wish to return to an item for further consideration, check it on the test booklet, not on the answer sheet.

5. Avoid glancing frequently at the clock. This not only wastes time but breaks concentration.

6. Other time-consuming mannerisms include glancing frequently at the instructor, polishing glasses, examining fingernails, gazing at wall or ceiling, and pampering oneself with excessive yawning and stretching.

MONDAY–MORNING QUARTERBACKING

Instead of becoming despondent over a low grade, sit down calmly and find out where you went wrong. Your returned examination paper can be a valuable guide to learning. Recognize your errors, analyze them, and learn how to correct them. Above all, study any comments made by the instructor; and if you have further questions, ask him. You may find that your trouble is not knowing how to take examinations more than lack of knowledge.

The most impressive thing you can do in any course is to show steady progress. Few instructors give a term grade based on a cumulative average. The last examination in a course is usually far more important than the first. Consider, if you were a professor, which of the following two students you would give the higher mark. Student A starts with an 85, dips to 75, rises slightly to 80, and on his final exam staggers through with a 72. Student B fails his first test with a 60, pulls up to 75, then to 80, and is a class leader with a 90 on his final. A student's steady progress reflects credit on both himself and his instructor.

Writing Themes and Course Papers*

Besides requiring you to read more than you have ever done before, your college work will also require you to write more. Rare is the student who does not spend many hours each term writing "papers": themes, essays, research papers, critiques, and reports. Although most writing in the first year centers in the Freshman English course, every subject will make some demands on your writing skills. Even in the physical and engineering sciences, where mathematical and symbolic expressions play so large a part in communication, there are laboratory experiments to write up and technical reports to prepare.

Papers for college courses run the full range from *themes* written primarily out of your own experience and thinking to *research papers* based on thorough and systematic library research. Then there is the *report* on a specific project or experiment; and there is the *critical essay* for which you may do research but in which your subjective judgments, personal preferences, and tastes have fuller play than in the more rigorously objective research paper. If you are not sure what kind of paper you are expected to produce for a given assignment, ask your instructor.

The handbook or rhetoric used in the Freshman English course which most college students are required to take is your best handy source for information about the specific procedures and mechanics of organizing and writing papers. Besides being a reference book to consult on matters of grammar and punctuation, it will tell you how to use the library, how to find source materials for research papers, how to prepare a bibliography, take notes on cards, document your use of sources with appropriate footnotes, construct an outline, and put the whole thing together according to approved standards of form and style. Every student should own a composition handbook and cultivate the habit of referring to it regularly. It is not the purpose of this chapter to duplicate information which you will find in such a handbook, but to highlight a few of the most common problems that students come up against in writing papers.

* Adapted in part from material supplied by Ian D. Elliot.

WHAT TO WRITE ABOUT

Writing is communicating to a reader. It is not putting five hundred or a thousand words on paper to fulfill the conditions of a course assignment. If you keep this fact in mind, you will realize that the first essential is to choose a subject that really interests you and that you think you can make interesting to your reading audience (your instructor).

A practical plan is to keep a list of possible topics for themes. Reserve a page or two in your notebook, and jot down subjects and fleeting thoughts as they occur to you. The very fact that you are building such a list will sharpen your awareness of the theme materials in your everyday life, in your recollections of the past, and in the ideas that are suggested to you by people you talk with and books you read. Look over your list from time to time, and think about the topics. When some incident in your experience or some item in your reading ties up with one of them, note that down too. In this way you can build up a nice little fund of ideas to draw on when you have a theme to write. To have at least a starting point is a great psychological advantage.

Part of the question "What to write about?" is "What's worth writing about?" Starting, for example, with the idea of writing a theme about your summer as a camp counselor, you could probably produce a respectable enough paper on "A Camp Counselor's Day" or "The Duties of a Camp Counselor"; but honestly, would either you or your instructor feel a spark of real interest in such a theme? And yet a summer as a camp counselor certainly must have yielded material well worth writing about. If you are interested in your subject and in getting it across to your reader, you will try to convey what it *means to you;* you will try to express how you, as an individual, interpret an experience or an idea. To have something worth writing about you don't have to have had world-shaking experiences and you don't have to express yourself on great and noble subjects. But you do have to have something that is particularly yours to say, no matter how commonplace the materials from which it emerges. If, from your summer camp experience, you decide to write on why twelve-year-olds are (or are not) your favorite age-group, or how you have come to feel that you are (or are not) meant for a teaching career, you will have something worth saying, for the simple reason that it will bear the stamp of *your* mind and personality, and to that extent will be original.

In the same way, when you choose a subject for a research paper, remember that you are going to put in a lot of time looking up books and articles in the library, reading the materials you find, and thinking about them. And if you pick any old topic, it can be just that — putting in time. But if you choose a topic which you actually would like to know more about, a topic that ties up with a live interest, you will experience a real zest in tracking down information and will enjoy communicating your findings to your reader.

FIVE HUNDRED WORDS, OR MORE, OR LESS

Most writing assignments are made in terms of a number of words — a theme of 250 words, or 500 words, or a research paper of 2000 words, and so on. Unfortunately, the purpose of this requirement is all too often misunderstood. The student focuses his attention on getting words down on paper until the magic number is reached, in much the same spirit that he would turn on a faucet and let it run until he had a pint, a quart, or a gallon of water as needed. The catch is that you can't put a gallon of water into a pint measure, or fill up a gallon measure with a pint.

One of the commonest faults in freshman papers is the choice of a topic that is too ambitious for the length of the paper and the time available for it. The result is a paper full of generalities: a few vague statements that are not developed, supported, illustrated, and interrelated, as they should be in good expository writing. Then, to compound the error, if a word count shows that the paper is running short, the writer hopefully inserts an extra sentence here and a phrase there until his goal of so many words is reached. By ignoring the significance of the word requirement, he has got himself into a situation where he can only skim the surface of his subject, and by looking at wordage as an end in itself he has been tempted into "padding."

The right way is to make the required number of words an integral part of your choice of a topic. If you are assigned a 2000-word research paper, and have six weeks to prepare it in, you can obviously tackle a bigger subject and cover it in more detail than you could in a 300-word theme due in a week. On the other hand, a topic that you could handle pleasantly in 250 words might not be worth drawing out to a thousand. Suppose, for example, you are interested in the general subject of "Railroads." For a paper of 2000 words, you might write on some rather broad aspect of railroading, such as "The Decline of Passenger Service Since World War II," or "Railroads: The Case for (or against) Public Subsidies," or "The Role of Railroads in the Civil War." For a theme of about 500 words, you would choose a more limited aspect: perhaps "An Experiment That Failed," or "Monorail: Railroad of the Future?" A 250-word paper would call for a very narrowly defined topic, such as an anecdote or an incident: "Wrong Train!" or "A Famous Locomotive," or "Model-Railroad Fan." It may take a little practice at first, but you will soon get so you can readily adjust the focus of a topic to the given length and the available time.

KEEPING TO THE POINT

Writing about something other than your stated topic is like misinterpreting a question on an examination, except that a misguided paper wastes a lot more time and energy. This applies both to papers for which the topic or exact title has been assigned by the instructor and to those for which you choose your own subject and title. But there is an important distinction.

When the topic is assigned, you must deal with facts and ideas specifically related to it. If an interesting bypath opens up, make a note of it on your list of possible topics for future use, but don't let it entice you away from your main point in *this* paper. Keep asking yourself: "Does this really pertain to the subject I am writing about? Is it contributing to my purpose as defined in the title and thesis statement?"

If, however, you are choosing your own subject, you have a little more leeway; for as you think about your topic, do research on it, or otherwise "work into" it, you may wish to change your approach or emphasis. The student who begins by selecting as his topic "Religious Influences in the Plays of Eugene O'Neill" may find, after some preliminary reading and research, that the primary influences were not religious but psychological. Another student who has started with the thought of writing on the effects of the automobile on American life may become so fascinated with changing trends in the design and styling of cars that he decides to write his paper on that topic instead. This is all part of the process of limiting and focusing, but once you have settled into your topic you should be sure that everything in your paper contributes to its development and that your final title accurately reflects the contents.

ORGANIZING YOUR MATERIALS

An interesting topic, original ideas, and a wealth of supporting details and information — these are the ingredients of a good paper, but they add up to nothing without good organization.[1] To order your materials, first prepare a brief statement of the thesis, purpose, or scope of your paper — not necessarily in the exact words you will use in your final version, but a definite statement, as precise as you can make it, to serve as a point of reference and keep you on the track. Next make an outline. This will help you think your materials through, decide on the order in which you can best present them, see how your main points relate to the whole topic and to each other, and plan on the most effective use of your supporting materials or other details. Now you are ready to write your first draft.

GETTING STARTED: THE FIRST DRAFT

For most students, once they have decided on a topic, the hardest part of a theme or course paper is beginning the actual writing. The best way to get started is to start. Don't sharpen any more pencils, don't go to the library for one last item of information, don't rationalize that you can make a better start tomorrow. Tell yourself that this is the zero hour, and that you will have something to show for it when you get up from your desk. Even if you make a false start and have to discard and begin over, you will have made the plunge and will be mentally set to write. Sometimes the

[1] Refer to Chapter 3 for the elements and basic types of coherent organization.

introduction is a stumbling block. You may find it helpful, as many writers do, to start with the body of the paper, and come back to the introduction later when you can see it in better perspective.

With your outline before you, write as rapidly and spontaneously as you can. Don't strive, on this first draft, for gemlike perfection of sentences and paragraphs. Your aim at this point is to get your ideas and information down on paper. If you have constructed a careful outline, thought about your topic, and done a conscientious job of research (if research is necessary for the kind of paper you are writing), you should be able to produce a first draft that in substance and general organization is reasonably close to what you want to say. True, it is likely to be a very rough draft — messy with deletions, insertions, and scribbled afterthoughts. But now you have something tangible to work with.

When you have finished your first draft, read it through. Make notes of any points you have left out, any new thoughts that come to you as you read, or any places where you would like to make changes or improvements. Now, while all these matters are fresh in your mind, make a clean copy, incorporating as much revision as you conveniently can. Don't worry too much at this stage about word-choice, spelling, and punctuation. Deal first with the larger problems of organization and development; you can tackle stylistic matters later.

REVISING

Lay your paper aside for a day or so; let it cool off, and *then* read it over critically, putting yourself as closely as you can in your reader's place. Will points that are so clear to you be equally clear to him? Do your sentences say exactly what you want them to mean? Have you stuck to the topic, and does everything contribute in some way to its development? Or have you wandered into byways that might better be explored in another paper? Is there a logical progression from paragraph to paragraph, and from point to point; and is this progression made sufficiently clear by transitional devices? Perhaps you will even feel that some change in the order of presenting the materials would result in a stronger paper. What about balance in the presentation of main points: have you used too little supporting material in some instances, too much in others? A serious flaw in many student papers is a failure to *develop* ideas, a tendency to deal in flat statements and generalizations. Whether you want to convey an experience or sensation (the beauty of the campus in October) or a thesis or intellectual concept (the Versailles Treaty as the seedbed of World War II), you will be successful in doing so only if you give your reader the concrete and specific details on which your general conclusions are based. Generalizations are like skeletons; specifics are the flesh and blood and living tissue of effective writing.

The advantage of a cooling-off period of at least twenty-four hours between the first draft and a re-reading and revision is that your mind has now

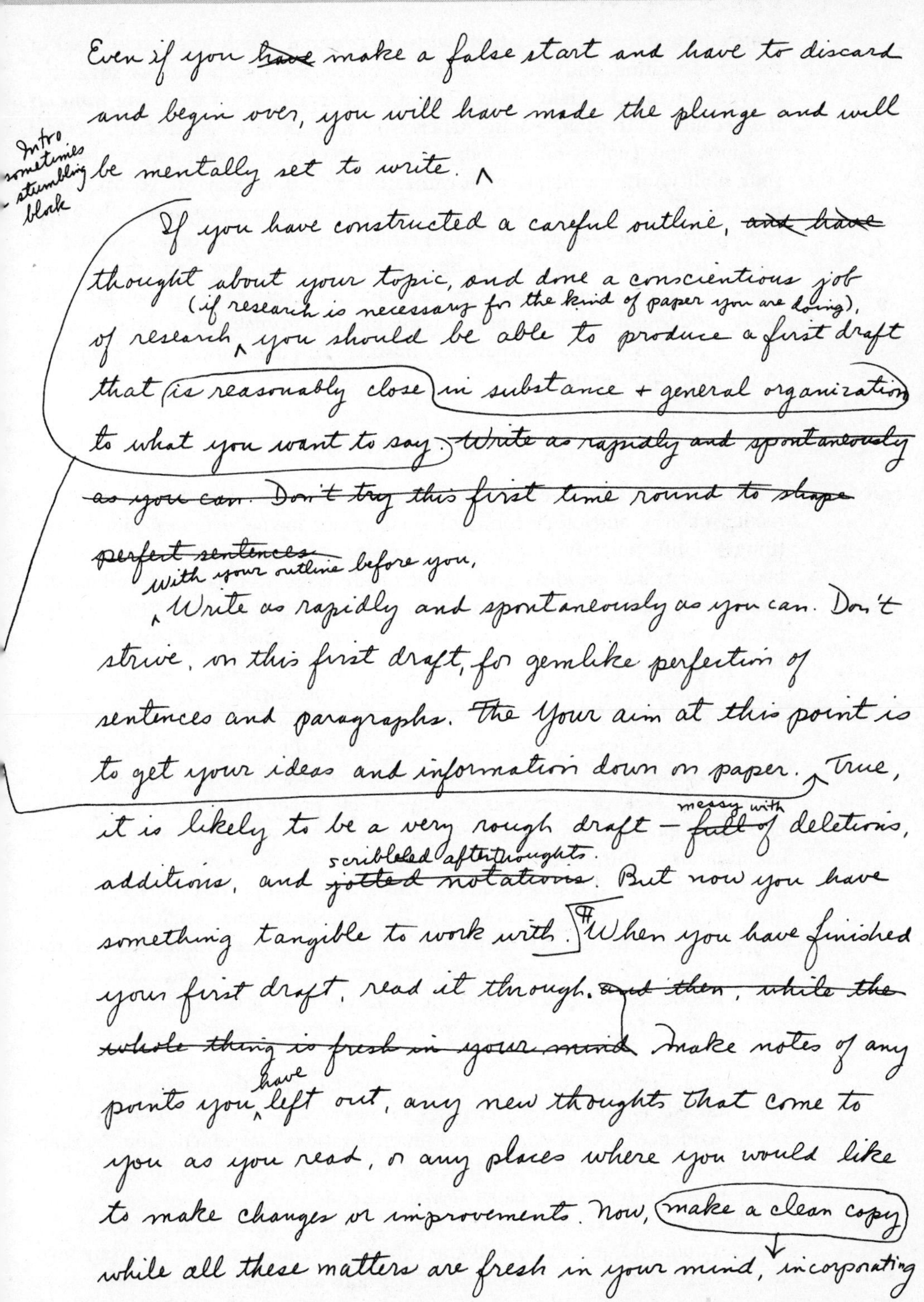

Even if you ~~have~~ make a false start and have to discard and begin over, you will have made the plunge and will

Intro sometimes ~ stumbling block

be mentally set to write. ∧

If you have constructed a careful outline, ~~and have~~ thought about your topic, and done a conscientious job of research ∧ (if research is necessary for the kind of paper you are doing), you should be able to produce a first draft that (is reasonably close) (in substance + general organization) to what you want to say. ~~Write as rapidly and spontaneously as you can. Don't try this first time round to shape perfect sentences.~~

With your outline before you,

∧ Write as rapidly and spontaneously as you can. Don't strive, on this first draft, for gemlike perfection of sentences and paragraphs. ~~The~~ Your aim at this point is to get your ideas and information down on paper. ∧ True, it is likely to be a very rough draft — ~~full of~~ messy with deletions, additions, and ~~jotted notations~~ scribbled afterthoughts. But now you have something tangible to work with. ⁋ When you have finished your first draft, read it through. ~~and then, while the whole thing is fresh in your mind~~ make notes of any points you ∧have left out, any new thoughts that come to you as you read, or any places where you would like to make changes or improvements. Now, (make a clean copy) while all these matters are fresh in your mind, ∨ incorporating

FIGURE 12-1

Page from a First Draft

dropped the intimate associations with the material which were established in the act of writing, and you can more easily spot flaws such as those suggested above. You may be lucky enough, for a short theme, to get what you want on the second draft. For a long paper, you may need to go through several revisions and cooling-off periods. When you have solved, to the best of your ability, any problems of organization and development, go over your paper with an editorial eye for sentence structure, paragraphing, clarity of expression, choice of words, punctuation, spelling, and other stylistic or mechanical matters. When you are satisfied that you have done the best job you can, make a final "fair copy" to hand in, typewritten if possible, but neatly and legibly handwritten if not. Be sure to give this a final reading for any careless errors: misspellings, mistakes in punctuation, words omitted in copying, and the like.

AVOIDING PLAGIARISM

Plagiarism is to the realm of words and ideas what shoplifting, embezzlement, robbery, and other forms of stealing are to the realm of money and things. Unfortunately, the parallel between the misappropriation of somebody else's words or ideas and of somebody else's wallet is not sufficiently recognized, and a student who wouldn't dream of helping himself to another person's tangible property is not always as careful about ownership rights in the things of the mind.

A college student who deliberately copies words written by someone else, and passes them off as his own, knows perfectly well what he is doing, and must be left to his own conscience. He might also keep in mind the fact that any instructor will very soon notice discrepancies in style, method of approach, and level of performance between one paper and another, as well as between papers prepared outside class and written work done in class or on examinations. Purposeful stealing is as stupid as it is wrong.

Most students, of course, won't do this kind of thing. But there is another kind of plagiarism into which even the best-intentioned student may fall simply because he doesn't understand the use of source materials and the conventions and obligations of scholarship. He is, however, expected to learn responsible practices, and he will be held accountable for lapses through ignorance, even if not in the same degree as for lapses through intent.

In research papers, of course, you *must* make use of the findings of others; that, indeed, is one of the purposes of research — to support a thesis by citing evidence (facts, ideas, and interpretations) obtained from various sources. All that is required is that you acknowledge every such citation in a footnote which refers the reader to the source.

There are two kinds of borrowing: the use of the actual words of the source (quoting) and the use of the substance or ideas restated in your own words (paraphrasing). Both require footnote acknowledgment. When you quote, you enclose the material in quotation marks or set it apart from the text by spacing and indention. The quotation should be given *exactly* as it appears in the source. If you omit anything, you should show that you have done so by inserting three dots (points of ellipsis); and if you add anything, such as a clarifying word or comment of your own, you should enclose it in square brackets. It is therefore very important, when you are taking notes on your reading for a research paper, to enclose in quotation marks any passages, phrases, or single significant words taken directly out of the source; otherwise you may later believe that the note is a restatement in your own words, and fail to show it as a direct quotation in your paper.

Unless you have been extremely careless in taking notes on your reading, quotations should give you no trouble; but students sometimes are confused about their obligation to a source when they do not use its exact words. When you paraphrase — that is, restate, boil down, or in any other way borrow substance or ideas — you are just as much obligated to cite your source as though you were directly quoting; for restatement in your own words does not make another person's material yours. Only if the information you use is a matter of general knowledge (facts, for example, that may be found in a number of books) *and in addition* is written wholly in your words — only then are you justified in not giving a specific source.

Abundant and conscientious documentation in a research paper is not a confession of lack of originality. The more thorough and scholarly the treatment of a topic, the more exhaustive is the search into and use of sources. Originality lies in the use you make of your findings, in your thinking about them, your interpretation of them, the connections you make and the conclusions you draw. This part of the paper is your own. You use and cite sources, in other words, as evidence to substantiate *your* development of *your* thesis.

A FINAL WORD

If a student is going to achieve in college, he not only *can* learn to write acceptable papers — he *must!* To some, good writing comes more easily than to others; but any student is capable of writing "well" to the extent of producing papers which *cover what they set out to cover, and accomplish this in language that is precise, clear, and grammatically correct.* Your instructor expects this much of you; he does not expect you to be a Henry James, a J. D. Salinger, or a James Thurber.

A theme or a course paper, like genius, is one-tenth inspiration and nine-tenths perspiration. So don't depend on inspiration. In fact, an early start is so important that you may be able through this means alone to get a better grade than you otherwise would. For an early start permits you to choose a topic thoughtfully, do any necessary limiting or expanding while there is still plenty of time, write as many drafts as you need to, and finally to revise and polish until your finished paper represents what you are really capable of doing.

13

Speeches and Oral Reports

by James A. Wood

In college you will almost certainly be called on to give speeches or other oral presentations from time to time. And if the prospect doesn't exactly kindle you with joyful anticipation, you are not alone. Most students are likely to approach a formal speaking situation with some degree of nervous dread, even when the audience is made up of classmates whom they see every day. Yet the ability to speak effectively before a group is not a difficult skill to develop, and it is one that will serve you well, whatever your sphere of activity, all your life.

It should hearten you to realize that even the experienced and successful speaker may feel apprehensive before giving a speech. But he has learned to convert nervous tension into constructive energy that actually helps him to be alert, vigorous, and effective in speaking. To make tension work for you, rather than against you, you must be (1) fully prepared to do your job, and (2) motivated by a strong and sincere desire to communicate to your audience. This means knowing your subject well, taking ample time to think about and plan what you will say, evaluating your topic in terms of your intended listeners, concentrating on what you can give them of interest and value — in a word, being audience-minded instead of self-centered. This mental attitude will have a bearing on your speech at all stages, from planning through the moment of delivery.

THE PLAN FOR THE SPEECH

The ideal finished plan for a speech or oral report is a very detailed outline, usually containing 30 to 50 per cent as many words as the actual speech. It is thus much fuller than an outline for a written paper, but far from being your speech word for word. From it you can see the order and relationship of ideas, distinguish main ideas from supporting materials, and note where the major junctures or transitions come. It enables you to learn the speech as a complete, organized pattern of ideas, and thus to avoid the rote memorization which often results in a parrot-like delivery.

Basic parts of the outline. The outline may conveniently be divided into four basic parts: introduction, purpose statement, body, and conclusion.

1. *Introduction.* In the introduction you seek to win the *good will, attention,* and *interest* of your listeners. Your means to this end are a pleasant, confident delivery, and such devices as a striking example, an interesting but relevant narrative, or relating the topic to something the audience is already interested in. The introduction should also provide any *background information* the audience is likely to need: definitions of important terms, or appropriate historical or social context.

2. *Purpose statement.* Your statement of purpose, often no more than a single sentence, tells your audience just what ground you intend to cover. This statement should be clearly and precisely worded, because it provides a focus for the entire speech. Usually it comes at or near the end of the introduction.

3. *Body.* The body or main part of the speech should comprise between 65 and 90 per cent of the whole. Here you develop the topic presented in your purpose statement.

4. *Conclusion.* The conclusion is essentially a summary of the main points made in the body of the speech. It also gives you an opportunity to round off the speech smoothly by referring to something mentioned in the introduction, by suggesting broader implications, or by specifically relating speech to audience.

Components of the speech. A speech may be thought of as a fusion of main ideas, supporting materials, and transitions. A good speaker gives deliberate attention to each of these components separately and in combination.

1. *Main or key ideas.* A shrewd speaker will not expect his audience to remember a welter of details. Rather, he has a few key ideas he wants to convey (for example, the four main stages in building a house, or five characteristics of Hemingway's prose style), and he constructs his speech so as to help the audience grasp and remember them. He may hope some of the audience will note and remember subordinate points also, but he regards these primarily as means of making his key ideas clearer and more memorable.

You must first, then, have a precise idea of the main points you wish to put across and the best order in which to present them. On these points you build your outline, making sure that every item in the body of the speech contributes to developing a particular main idea. In this way you insure against confusing your audience by digressing or backtracking.

2. *Supporting materials.* Supporting materials help your listeners to understand, accept, and remember your main ideas. They provide evidence for the main points, relate the subject to the knowledge and experience of the audience, and maintain interest. They are used in greater quantity and variety in speaking than in writing to give the audience a chance to absorb

and accept the main points; for unlike the reader, the listener cannot stop to ponder or look back.

Whereas main ideas are likely to be general statements, supporting materials should be specific: *factual data,* such as names, dates, places, and events; *examples,* ranging from brief references to detailed anecdotes; *vivid description* of how things look, feel, sound, smell, taste; *comparison and contrast* with things familiar to the audience; *expert testimony or opinion,* cited or quoted; *literary quotations,* when they are apt. *Statistics* can be useful, but must be handled with care since they are harder to take in by ear than by eye. If they can be translated into concrete or pictorial terms, so much the better; thus, in addition to stating the estimated gallons of water wasted by a community's leaky plumbing over a period of time, you might give the time it would take the same volume of water to pour over Niagara Falls.

A special type of supporting material is the *visual aid,* which covers a wide range of materials, including blackboard or chartboard drawings, poster-type materials displayed on an easel, three-dimensional models, specimens, and films. Visual aids are useful in holding the audience's attention and in presenting statistical relationships (as in graphs) and complicated structures or processes which are hard to explain in words alone. Though experienced speakers sometimes draw or write as they talk, a beginner would be wise to prepare in advance any aids he intends to use and thus avoid having to do two things at once.

3. *Transitions.* Transitions help emphasize your main ideas and enable your audience to move mentally with you from one point to the next. If your transitions are not unmistakably clear, your listeners will become confused. Inexperienced speakers often fail to realize that oral presentation requires far more transitional material than writing does, and that oral transitions must be more obvious and repetitive than those used in writing.

Oral transitions may take a number of forms. First, you may emphasize main ideas by *restatement,* saying them twice, in different words. This gives your hearers a better chance, a little more time, to grasp these ideas and to see that they are relatively important.

Another transitional device is *pre-outlining.* Near the beginning of your speech, perhaps right after the purpose statement, you may tell your audience the main points you intend to take up. Similarly, at the beginning of each major section, after stating the main idea, you may outline the ground you intend to cover.

If you have several sections of parallel nature and importance, you may make use of *listing:* either enumeration ("First . . . ," "Second . . . ," etc.) or a key phrase repeated with the introduction of each main idea, or a combination of both ("The first type of jet engine is . . . ," "The second type of jet engine is. . . .").

Connective transitions tell your audience that you are moving on to a new section of your speech and indicate how it is related to the previous one.

For example, "Now that we understand the problem that faced the engineer, let's see how he solved it." Or, " Since we now know the history of this riot, let's attempt to identify its underlying causes."

Finally, in *internal summaries* you can condense and restate some or all of the points you have already presented.

MAKING YOUR OWN SPEECH PLAN

Choosing a topic. Many speakers get off to a bad start by selecting a topic that is too broad. Remember that in ten minutes of speaking you can cover the equivalent of only five to seven typewritten pages, and that supporting materials and transitions should take up a proportionately larger part of an oral presentation than of a written one. Usually a speaker should not try to get more than three or four main points across in a short speech of ten or fifteen minutes. It is the depth of perceptive explanation, interpretation, and illustrative detail, rather than the amount of ground covered, that determines the value of a speech.

Consider the interests of the audience and the demands of the occasion, but also pick a topic you are really interested in. Your interest, or lack of it, will be sensed by your listeners and will influence their reception of what you have to say.

Phrase your topic in one simple sentence, to serve as a tentative purpose statement, and analyze it to see if it is clearly focused.

Preliminary overview. Ransack your mind for information, ideas, and opinions on the topic and for ideas about further sources of information. List all these items, and use the list as a guide in gathering further information. If you start from what *you* know and think, your own personality will emerge in the speech and thereby provide some original flavor and perhaps even a fresh outlook on the topic.

Break your subject down into the main areas or ideas you want to cover. Your topic statements for each of these will become the main headings in your outline for the body of your speech.

Research. From the list of items you made in your preliminary overview, you can decide what material you must obtain from the library or other sources of information. But don't overlook your own experience and imagination as a resource, especially for such supporting materials as analogies, comparisons, and actual or hypothetical examples. Always keep the needs of your audience in mind.

Preparation of final outline. The purpose statement, as the focus, should be at least tentatively planned at an early stage of your preparation. The introduction and conclusion are usually planned after the body of the speech — unless you get an inspired idea while you are doing research or working on the main part.

The outline for the body of the speech should be taking shape around your main headings while you are doing your research. When you have all your material together, plan the *exact phrasing* of your statements of main ideas and transitions, just as you intend to say them in your speech. Write these in full in the appropriate places in the outline. Now insert your supporting materials as sub-entries under the appropriate main headings, but don't write them out in full as you did the main statements and transitions — a few words of reminder are enough. If you overlook any main ideas or transitions, your whole structure may come crashing down. But if you slip up on a supporting detail or two, the consequences are not serious; and your delivery will have a more spontaneous quality if you develop them from notes rather than from pre-planned sentences.

At least two days before you are to give your speech, go over your outline to put it in final form. Many speeches fail to achieve their full potential just because the speaker does not take the trouble to make a final check for subordination of supporting materials to main points, clarity of transitions, and deletion of irrelevant material.

PREPARING TO DELIVER THE SPEECH

First, read your outline through several times, both silently and aloud. Your aim is to learn the pattern or sequence of ideas, not to memorize words and sentences. To fix the pattern in your memory, test yourself with such questions as, "What are my main points?" "How do I explain my third main idea?" "What transition do I use after the section on . . . ?"

Next, say your speech aloud a few times, referring to your outline when necessary. (Time yourself to be sure you meet the requirements.) Keep thinking in terms of ideas, not of set phrases and sentences. Remember that oral speech patterns are more conversational and less formal than written ones.

Now prepare to "go it alone" without your outline, as you must do in the actual speech situation. You may, however, plan on using conventional speaking notes — a very much abbreviated outline, of words and phrases, typed or written on 4 × 6-inch cards. These notes will help you keep to your plan but will not tempt you into reading, as your full outline might.

The practice delivery. With your outline well in mind and your note cards in hand, you are ready to practice delivering your speech. Try to duplicate the actual speaking situation as closely as possible. Ideally, you would practice your speech in the room or hall where you are to give it, with a few friends serving as audience. This is your chance to anticipate the physical "feel" of speech-making. Pay conscious attention to your gestures and voice; think about what you are going to do with your hands; use your speaking notes so you will be accustomed to them; speak loud enough to be heard at the back of the room; assume an alert and confident bearing.

Go through the speech from beginning to end. If you make mistakes, keep right on going — you can give special attention to troublesome parts later. Some students can get by with one or two trial runs; others need ten or a dozen. Practice is more valuable if spread over two or three days. Even for a simple class report, avoid the temptation to practice only at the last minute or not at all. The more attention you give to techniques of delivery in practice sessions, the less they will throw you off your stride in your actual presentation.

FACING THE AUDIENCE

No matter how much you practice, there are some things that can be worked out only in the actual speaking situation. An effective speaker is sensitive to the response of his listeners and responds in turn to them. He is both stimulated and cued by his audience, alert to the need to make minor adjustments in his presentation: for example, to slow down and insert internal summaries, if his hearers seem confused; or to omit some supporting material and get on to the next point, if they seem restless.

An important element in this establishment of *rapport* is good eye contact with the audience. You should appear to be in a genuine two-way relationship with your listeners, and this is impossible if you are examining the ceiling or the floor, or staring fixedly at your notes or your hands. When you talk with an individual, you look directly at him; and you should do the same with your audience. You can start by establishing eye contact with a single person. Look directly and pleasantly at him, and address yourself to him until you feel that you have his full attention and have established a relationship. Repeat with one or more other individual members of the audience; then, when you have gained confidence, pick out a *group* of persons, and look and speak directly at them, as a unit. Do the same with other groups in different parts of the room. In this way, you can learn to establish eye contact with the audience as a whole.

Many of the mannerisms that inhibit full communication with an audience are the result of undirected nervous tension. A few deep breaths can do wonders to steady pulse and voice and put you in physical control of the situation. Your physical bearing has a direct effect on your audience's response. If you sag or lean against a desk or speaking stand, you will suggest apathy and dullness to your listeners. If you fiddle with a pencil or a ring or your note cards, their attention will be diverted from what you are saying. Stand erect, and make a conscious effort to control any overflow motion generated by nervousness, or else convert it into expressive gestures.

In the same way, your voice cues the audience. First of all, you must speak loudly and clearly enough to be heard and understood. Vary your rate and pitch to hold the attention and interest of your listeners. If you clip rapidly along in an even, monotonous tone of voice, you will suggest that your main aim is to get the whole thing over as fast as possible and that what you have to say is of no particular interest anyway. As a rule, you should speak more slowly and formally when you are giving main ideas or difficult material, and more rapidly and conversationally when you are citing examples or narrating anecdotes. Don't be afraid of a pause. If you forget what comes next, take time for an unhurried look at your notes. If the right word won't come, don't panic and try to fill up the silence with "uh, uh," but pause without embarrassment until you are able to resume. Good speakers, in fact, make deliberate use of pauses to emphasize important points or to recapture an audience's wandering attention.

AN ORAL PRESENTATION OF A WRITTEN REPORT

In some classes you may be asked to make an oral presentation of a paper which you are also to hand in as a written report. This can present a problem for two reasons: (1) oral discourse, as we have seen, differs from written discourse in several significant ways; (2) the required length of the written report may be incompatible with the amount of class time available for giving it orally.

There are three ways of solving the problem:

1. You can write your paper and then use it as source material to prepare an oral report. The disadvantage of this solution is that it requires you to prepare two distinct reports, one written and one oral.

2. You can write the paper with the idea of oral presentation primarily in mind. But this has disadvantages too. For one thing, *writing* oral discourse is a rather specialized skill. Moreover, the very things that help make the oral presentation a success — the restatement and repetition, the numerous and obvious transitions, the relative amount of space given to the supporting materials, the personal quality and conversational tone — may be criticized as flaws in the formal written report.

3. Probably the best plan is to write the report as you normally would, and then *adapt* it to oral presentation. On a clean carbon copy, note down the supplementary supporting materials, internal summaries, and emphatic transitions you intend to add when you give the report orally. By merely noting these items, rather than writing them out in full, you have a chance to work in some conversational spontaneity. Practice reading the paper aloud until you know it well and will be able to look up from it frequently to establish eye contact with your audience. The more familiar you are with the sentence rhythms, the better you will be able to adapt them to a spoken delivery. Know exactly where the supplementary oral materials come, and practice moving smoothly from reading to speaking and back to reading again.

14

Study Hints for Language Students

by William G. Moulton

Language teachers are constantly working on new methods to help students learn foreign languages as efficiently and thoroughly as possible. You will find their efforts reflected in the textbooks you use and in the type of classroom instruction you receive. But textbooks and teaching methods are only part of the story — usually, in fact, just about one-third of the story. For if we accept the traditional rule-of-thumb that a college student should average two hours of outside study for each hour of classroom work, this means that you are on your own for two-thirds of the time.

The following study hints are offered in the hope that they will enable you to work more efficiently during the unsupervised two-thirds of your foreign language time. They offer no magic answer, no patent pill that will make everything easy and painless; they are merely meant to help you in your *work*. However, since most students approach the study of a foreign language from precisely the wrong point of view, some at least of the following remarks should be of help to you. There is no one set of suggestions which will fit all students perfectly, and experience will show just which techniques are most useful in your own particular case.

LEARNING TO SPEAK A FOREIGN LANGUAGE

You can't learn a language by "thinking" about it. Nearly all the non-language work which a college student does involves (or should involve) a large amount of thinking. Of course, you are asked to read a certain amount of material and to learn a certain number of facts; but this is only the beginning. The most important thing for you to do is to go home, sit down, and *think* about these facts: organize them, analyze them, and interpret them. Most students are so accustomed to this "thinking" approach that they try to learn a new language in the same way; the results are always disastrous.

A language is a set of habits. All of us speak our native language with complete fluency. Since we learned this one language so extremely well, it is worth while considering just how we did it. It is obvious from the very start that we didn't do it by "thinking." We had almost completely mastered the sounds and structure of the language by the time we were five or six years old, and at that time we couldn't "think" anywhere near as well as we can now that we are adults with an expensive education behind us. Instead of "thinking," we just listened to other people and copied what they said. By doing this over and over again, we eventually built up the complicated sets of habits which now let us talk our native language with complete ease. The "thinking" which we now do when we talk is concerned almost entirely with *what* we are going to say (the content), rather than with *how* we are going to say it (the language). We don't "think" about saying *he works* (with an ending -*s*) but *they work* (with no ending); nor do we "think" about pronouncing the word *the* as *thee* before words beginning with a vowel ("the apple, the orange"), but as *thuh* before words beginning with a consonant ("the peach, the banana"). Complicated things like this have become completely matters of habit. Most of us don't even know we do them until somebody points them out to us.

You've got to listen and imitate. As adults trying to learn a foreign language, we face much the same job that we did as children learning our native language. We can't use quite the same methods, but the general approach will still be the same; we've got to listen to someone who knows how to speak the language, and we've got to imitate him as exactly as we can. In one way we're worse off than children: they start with a clean slate, whereas we're going to find that our native language habits get in the way all the time. But in another way we have a distinct advantage: since we already know one language, we can be told how the new language is put together, how it works, and how it differs from our native language. These directions ("grammar") can speed up the learning process considerably. Their only use, however, is to help us imitate more successfully; they are not an aim in themselves.

You've got to memorize. If a language is a set of habits, the only way to learn the language is to learn these habits. And you don't learn habits by "thinking"; you learn them by practice, practice, practice. In all your other courses you are asked to go home and organize, analyze, and interpret factual data; in your language course you will have to go home and practice the material you've heard in class over and over again until it becomes second nature. It's as simple — and as hard — as that.

Study out loud. One way to memorize the new material would be to read it over silently, again and again. That would be pretty ridiculous, of course, since you would then be learning not the language itself, but only the way it is symbolized on paper. In addition, it would be enormously inefficient. In reading silently, you would be using only your visual memory. If you study out loud, on the other hand, you first double your efficiency by adding auditory memory; then, by adding motor memory, you at least quadruple it, because motor memory is the most efficient of all. (Motor memory, you may recall, is the memory of what you do with your muscles. Proof of its efficiency is the fact that nobody ever forgets how to ride a bicycle, even though he may have had a terrible time learning it in the first place.) So do your language studying out loud. Of course, your roommate is going to think you're crazy when he walks in and finds you mumbling to yourself. But pay no attention to him; he probably has some peculiar habits too.

Divide the material into small units. As children, we were all good at memorizing; as adults, we have had most of this memorizing ability educated out of us. Hence a few comments on the technique of memorizing may be helpful. First of all, don't try to memorize a large body of material at once. Break it up into small units, memorize each of these units separately, and then string them all together.

Divide your study time into small units. If you spend two uninterrupted hours trying to memorize the material of a new lesson, you will do a poor job of memorizing and will probably go stark, raving mad in the process. Use a saner study technique. Start off with twenty minutes to half an hour at the most; then turn to some other work; then come back for another twenty minutes; and so on. Two hours divided into small bits like this will produce far better results than 120 straight minutes of agonizing study.

Go from the easy to the hard. Start off by reading the foreign language aloud right out of the book; generally you will have little trouble remembering how the new words sounded or what they meant. As soon as you have read a sentence in this way, look away from the book and say it again. Only after you have practiced a section of material like this several times should you go on to the really hard part: looking at the English and then trying to say the foreign language without peeking. If you have trouble saying a whole sentence in this way, try breaking it into smaller pieces, say each of them individually, and then string the pieces together.

Make full use of class hours. Smart students pack fifty minutes of practice into each class hour. When somebody else is reciting, they are mentally reciting right along with him, and hence have new material half memorized even before they go home to study it. If you just sit back and daydream until you are called on, you are not only wasting the class time you're paying for, but you are needlessly piling up extra future hours of study and review on the very materials that are being covered in class. (P.S. Don't let this get around, but we've known students who got through the course solely on the basis of what they learned during class hours, without doing a lick of outside work. We don't recommend this, and we don't consider such people very smart; but at least they weren't so dumb as to waste class time.)

Don't fall behind. Even though steady, day-by-day work is the best way to learn any subject, it is true that in many courses you *can* get yourself out of a jam by some high-pressure, last-minute cramming. Not so with a language. Cramming for a language exam would be about as sensible as cramming for a swimming test; you just can't learn habits that way. Furthermore, language learning is a highly cumulative process. It is like making a tower out of blocks: you keep building on top of what you did the day before. If you don't keep at the job steadily, pretty soon you're trying to put new blocks on top of empty space. So don't fall behind. Once in a while, of course, you won't have time to prepare an assignment. It happens — occasionally — in the best of families. But when it does happen, for heaven's sake don't be so bashful as to stay away from class. If you do, making up the work will be twice as hard. Come to class, tell the instructor you're unprepared, and learn as much as you possibly can from the classroom work.

Do you ever need to "think"? Yes; but in a very special way. Memorizing new material can hardly be called "thinking." But you will help yourself enormously if, as you memorize, you think about the grammatical explanations that go with each set of new material. The grammatical section of a new lesson may tell you, for example, about verb endings. After you have read this section, and have said the examples out loud, start memorizing the new material; and every time you say a verb form, fit it mentally into the scheme that has just been explained to you. This ability to think about the structure of the language is the one big advantage you have over a child; make full use of it.

LEARNING TO READ A FOREIGN LANGUAGE

How NOT to read. The following method is guaranteed to waste a maximum of time and to produce minimum results. Start off with the first sentence of the assignment, read along until you come to a word you don't know, and look it up in the vocabulary. Then read along to the next word you don't know, look *that* up in the vocabulary, etc., ad nauseam. By following this method you will need about four hours to cover the assignment, and by the time you're through you will have looked up so many different words that you will probably not remember a single one of them.

Translating versus reading. The goal you should aim for is the ability to pick up a foreign language book and understand what it is all about. You will never reach this goal by doing only word-for-word translation. Some of you may have had the experience of translating Latin in high school. The writer of these lines always got "A" in his high school Latin, and always delighted the teacher with his splendid translations. But at the end of four years he discovered that, though he could translate with the best of them, he was totally unable to sit down with a Latin book and read it for content. The reason was, of course, that nobody had ever made him *read* (as opposed to *translate*) Latin, and he was too stupid to realize that he should have done it for himself.

Intelligent guessing. If you are ever going to learn how to read for content, just about the most important skill for you to acquire is that of intelligent guessing, that is, figuring out what a word must mean because of the context in which it is used. We do this all the time in English. All of us know how to read a lot of words which we never use in speaking, or even in our own writing.

To deduce the meanings of words from their contexts — or, for that matter, to remember the meanings of words which you have looked up in the vocabulary — you will have to read them more than once. Let's suppose that you have 6 pages to read, and that on each page there are 10 words which you don't know. If you go through the 6 pages just once, and look up each of the 60 words, you surely won't be able to remember more than 10 of them. Instead of that, look up only 30 (a more manageable number) and make intelligent guesses for the remaining 30. Then, with the time that you have saved in this way, re-read the 6 pages at least two more times (preferably at intervals of several hours). In this way you may be able to remember as many as 25 of the 30 words which you looked up; and you will also have a pretty good idea of the meaning of the 30 which you did not look up. Score this way: 25 certain and 30 probable. And that's a lot better than only 10 certain.

How to get started. When you start out to do some reading in any foreign language, the cardinal rule to follow is this: *Never look a word up in the vocabulary until you have read the immediate context in which it occurs.* There is no sure way of knowing just how far you'll have to read to get the immediate context; it will vary from case to case. It would be idiotic to look up a word before reading through the whole sentence in which it occurs; some people prefer to read a whole paragraph, others a whole page or more. Perhaps the best over-all suggestion is this: read through the first sentence; and then keep on reading until you get lost. You may be able to follow along for a paragraph, or a page, or even the whole assignment.

What to do next. Let's assume that you've read through a paragraph before getting lost. Now go back to the beginning again, and read along until you come to the first word you can't reasonably guess at. Underline the word (so you can find it again quickly); look it up in the vocabulary; find the English translation which fits this sentence; put a pencil dot in the vocabulary margin beside the word (to show you've looked it up once); and then, turning back to the text, re-read the phrase in which the word occurs, trying to fix its meaning as you do so. Go through the first paragraph this way, looking up only the words you absolutely have to and making intelligent guesses at the others. Then tackle the following paragraphs in the same way, until you have read about half the assignment. At this point you will want to take a short break, if only to relieve the boredom. Lean back and stretch; and then, *re-read the pages you have just done.* This will use up only part of the time you have saved by making intelligent guesses, and it will do wonders. (The reason for doing it at this stage is that the whole section is still fresh in your memory, and a re-reading now will really tie down the loose ends. If you wait until later on, much of it will have grown cold.) Then go through the second half of the assignment, ending up with a re-reading again.

Trouble spots. Aside from words that you don't know, there are two other troubles you will run up against. First, there are the so-called "idioms": groups of words that mean more than the sum of their parts. Handle these just as you do single words: underline them, and look them up in the vocabulary, putting a pencil dot beside them there. Secondly, despite all the help that a vocabulary gives you, there will be passages here and there which you just can't understand. The most important thing to remember here is: *don't waste time on them.* If you can't understand such a passage the first time through, put a vertical line in the margin beside it, and read on ahead. Quite often you will pick up a clue later on, and the difficulty will be cleared up when you do the re-reading. But don't waste time on it even then. If, after a second honest try, you still can't figure out what it means, put a second vertical line in the margin, and ask your instructor to explain it to you when you come to class.

Nuisance words. The above method, besides helping you to read efficiently, carries with it a number of interesting by-products. The underlines automatically furnish you with a list of the words and idioms you had to look up; the single vertical lines in the margin show you which passages caused trouble the first time through; and the double vertical lines indicate the passages you had to ask your instructor about. All of this is extremely useful for reviewing later on. But perhaps most important of all are the dots you put in the vocabulary margin each time you look a word up. It is a well-known phenomenon that every reader has his own private set of nuisance words: words that he just can't seem to remember, and has to look up again and again. The dots in the vocabulary margin will automatically furnish you with a list of your own nuisance words. After you have read fifty pages or so of the book, run through the vocabulary and make a list of all the words that have more than two dots beside them. There won't be many such words; and if you spend a little extra time on them, you will save yourself a lot of vocabulary-thumbing later on.

Don't do it the hard way. The method outlined above is not the only way to read a foreign language, but we think it is probably the most efficient one. Traditionally, students have used three other general methods. The first is to write out a full English translation of everything. This is so wearisome a process that, fortunately, it has been followed by only a minute number of eager beavers. The second method is to make a list of all the words that have been looked up, together with their English translations. This is highly recommended for students who have time to kill and don't enjoy bridge or the movies; but, again, the sheer mechanical labor involved is out of all proportion to the benefits received. The third method is to write an English translation over each word that has been looked up in the vocabulary. This cuts down considerably on mechanical labor, but ultimately it defeats its own purpose: when you re-read such a passage, your eye will run along the printed line, skip up to read the translation, and never even see the foreign word which is what you are trying to learn in the first place. If you *must* write down the translation, at least do so in the margin, not between the lines of the text. This will certainly do no harm; but we doubt that it is worth the time and effort involved. However, you can suit yourself on this point.

IF YOU STILL HAVE TROUBLE . . .

In the long run, foreign language study boils down to a constant process of learning, forgetting a bit, re-learning, forgetting a little less, and re-learning again and again, until you begin to develop in the foreign language the same kinds of habits and skills that you already possess in English. The study hints given above should help you develop these habits and skills as efficiently as possible. As an added help, the textbooks you use will probably call for a considerable amount of review, and your instructor may add on some more. All of this should enable you to speak and read the language with reasonable fluency. If you still have trouble, the best suggestion we can make is that you do even more reviewing. Continue doing a conscientious job on each lesson as it is assigned; then spend a little extra time going over the material of past lessons. Quite often a little extra reviewing like this is all a person needs to catch up with the rest of the class.*

* This chapter is adapted, with permission, from an article of the same title which appeared in *The Modern Language Journal,* October, 1952. Since different teachers have varied approaches to the study of a language, Dr. Moulton does not expect total agreement with his ideas.

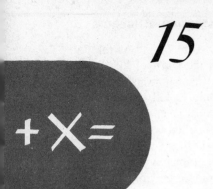

15

Hints on Studying Mathematics[*]

College work in mathematics is merely a continuation of a program that begins in the elementary grades with the first operations of arithmetic and continues through the junior and senior high schools with algebra, geometry, and trigonometry. No other subject in the curriculum has so long-sustained and cumulative a development, for at each stage in the program the student must be prepared to use all the mathematics he has studied previously. When students have difficulty with mathematics, it is almost always because they have not fully mastered some of the principles and processes, so that whenever they are called on to use these they are in trouble.

HOW TO REMEDY A WEAK BACKGROUND

If your background is shaky, what can you do about it? A thoroughgoing review is hardly feasible on top of your regular course load. There are, however, two practical ways to strengthen weak spots and fill in gaps.

First, you can attack each particular difficulty as it arises. Whenever you run into a need for a process or formula or principle that you don't understand, clear up that point so it won't bother you the next time. To accomplish spot review work of this kind, you should have right at hand textbooks covering arithmetic, algebra, geometry, and trigonometry — preferably those you used in secondary school and are familiar with. The fact that you have an immediate need for the material will now give you an incentive to master it. This is a good way to get the mathematical review you need for physics, chemistry, biology, astronomy, economics, and courses in the social sciences and education where statistical techniques are used. It is also a practical plan of attack if you are experiencing only occasional difficulties in your college mathematics course.

The second way to overcome weak spots in your background is a preventive measure: a systematic diagnosis of your mathematical competence. For this purpose, provide yourself with a "self-help" review book (your instructor

[*] Adapted from material supplied by Walter B. Carver and Harrison A. Geiselmann.

can recommend one) and work your way through it to discover what topics you need to study and to practice on.[1] By drill work with examples and problems in your particular area of difficulty you can forestall real trouble at a more advanced level.

The most common areas of weakness in arithmetic are fundamental operations with decimals and fractions, ratio and proportion, and percentage; in algebra, evaluation of expressions, fractions, fractional and literal equations, factoring, quadratic equations, and word problems; in trigonometry, logarithms.

DEVELOPING GOOD STUDY HABITS

In no field of study is the change from secondary school to college greater than in mathematics. In high school you probably did most of your drill work in class, under supervision, or as homework to be passed in for correction and credit. In college, however, you will have to get the equivalent of this drill by working out numerous exercises on your own — practicing those manipulations and operations which one masters only by doing them over and over again. And most of this "homework" you will not hand in for correction and credit. Your reward will be the proficiency that comes through hours of self-paced study, hours spent in working out exercises and problems and thinking your way to understanding.

There is a good reason for learning to be self-propelled in studying mathematics. In the context of modern life, mathematics is a very practical subject: it is all applied, or applicable. In an advanced course or in a job situation, there will not always be a teacher or a textbook at hand to tell you what process or formula to use. Mathematics can provide you with some powerful tools for achievement; but like all tools, they will be useful to you only if you know how to use them without having someone else guide your hand.

Keeping up to date. We have seen that mathematics — like a foreign language — is a cumulative subject, in which the student must be prepared at any point to use anything or everything he has previously learned; and further, that it is a subject in which drill and practice are required for the mastery of essential operations. For these reasons, it is absolutely necessary to keep your work up. If you fall behind, you'll find it terribly hard to catch up again, because you will be scanting the drill work which insures competence and understanding.

Taking notes in class. The general principles of note-taking discussed in Chapter 4 apply also to lectures and class discussions in mathematics.

---

[1] A good review workbook is *Basic Mathematics*, by M. Wiles Keller and James H. Zant (Boston: Houghton Mifflin Company; Form A, 1948; Form B, 1956). Each Form covers arithmetic, algebra, and trigonometry, and contains diagnostic tests from which the student can determine his strengths and weaknesses.

There are, however, some special things to keep in mind.

First, keep notes to a minimum. In courses involving quantitative relationships, the very process of note-taking hinders the student in following the instructor's line of argument. Record main ideas, but don't try to take down all the details and examples.

If the lectures are closely related to the textbook, you may find it helpful to read ahead before the lecture; you can then tell to what extent the lecture repeats and to what extent it supplements the text, and can take notes accordingly. You might even keep your textbook open and write supplementary or clarifying information right on the book page. But first check with your instructor to see whether he has any objections to your reading ahead or referring to the text during the class period.

If you lose the thread of a lecture or class discussion, or if you fail to understand a line of reasoning or a mathematical procedure, ask the instructor for clarification. Even if it's only a minor point at the time, failure to clear it up may lead you into major difficulties later. You'll have to do *your* part, though, by doing your advance preparation and giving the instructor your full attention during the class period.

To provide the maximum reinforcement for classtime learning, study your notes, and the related text material and problems, as soon after class as possible. But don't attempt any problems until you are sure you understand the material. Working at an assignment before you are ready for it wastes time — and, worse, may set you off on faulty procedures and thus interfere with understanding.

Studying for examinations. The best way to study for an examination is to keep your daily work up throughout the term. Then at examination time you can concentrate on polishing up what you have already learned.

Start early to review the problems you have had in assignments and previous tests, paying special attention to the more troublesome ones. This will give you a chance to ask help of your instructor, if you are still unsure of some procedures.

You may find the 3 × 5-inch card system useful for memorizing important formulas and principles which you will not be able to look up in the textbook during the examination. Record one such item to a card, and carry the cards around with you to study at odd moments. Be sure, however, that you understand the meaning of information which you memorize in this way, so that you could still work the problem even if you forgot the rote words and symbols. Think of a formula as a convenience or short cut, not as an end in itself.

Whenever you get back a test or examination, re-work the problems on which you made mistakes and find out what you did wrong. Correcting your errors is one of the most valuable learning experiences you can have, and is sure to have a bearing on your performance in subsequent tests.

PRACTICAL SUGGESTIONS FOR PROBLEM–SOLVING

Solving a mathematical problem is basically a two-part operation. First you have to analyze it, then you have to compute it. If you fail to size up the problem correctly, of course you can't compute your way to the correct solution. On the other hand, an error in calculation — whether from carelessness or from inadequate understanding of basic operations — can cancel out even a brilliant piece of analysis.

Set up the problem. To avoid the tendency toward trial-and-error and manipulation to get an answer, read the problem twice, carefully. Note what things are *given,* what principles and relationships are stated or implied, and what is to be found or proved. It may help you to jot these essentials down on a piece of paper. Now set the problem up. Don't think yet about computing it; concentrate first on analyzing it.

For example:

PROBLEM: How many minutes will it take a pump delivering 2.75 gal. per stroke and making 88 strokes per minute to pump 500 barrels of oil? (One barrel = 31.5 gal.)

Suggested set-up:

Let x = minutes required to pump 500 barrels of oil

$$\frac{500 \times 31.5}{2.75 \times 88} = x$$

Setting up the complete problem gives more opportunities for canceling, combining numbers, short-cut arithmetical processes, and other simplifications than you have when you do a problem in piecemeal fashion. Some instructors give partial credit on examinations if you can demonstrate your ability at least to set up the problem, even if you do not solve it correctly.

Draw a diagram. By drawing a careful diagram you can often clarify facts, principles, and relationships that are less evident from words alone. To illustrate:

PROBLEM: A pulley, 7 inches in diameter, is turning a belt and is rotating at 60 revolutions per minute (rpm). How fast is the belt moving in feet per minute? (Assume no slipping between the belt and the pulley.)

DIAGRAM:

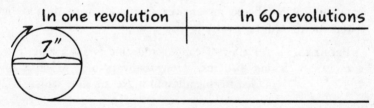

ANALYSIS FROM DIAGRAM:

When the pulley turns around once (1 rpm), it moves the belt a distance

$$C = \pi D = \frac{22}{7} \cdot \frac{7}{12} \text{ ft., or } \frac{11}{6} \text{ ft.}$$

In 60 revolutions, it would move the belt $\frac{11}{6}$ times 60, or 110 feet in a minute.

The complete set-up, then, and the solution, is:

$$\frac{22}{7} \cdot \frac{7}{12} \cdot 60 = 110 \text{ ft. per minute.}$$

Notice the advantage of setting up the entire problem, simplifying, and doing the calculation at the end, instead of computing as one goes along.

Apply your knowledge of arithmetic. 1. In algebra you can often use your knowledge of arithmetic to test a procedure about which you have doubts. Can you cancel as shown in the following?

$$\frac{a + b}{b} = a + 1$$

And does $\sqrt{a^2 + b^2} = a + b$?

By substituting several pairs of numbers for a and b, you can see that these statements are not generally true.

2. When the numbers involved in a problem are so large, so small, or so complicated that they interfere with your analysis of the problem, try temporarily substituting simpler numbers. In this way the nature of the problem is often more clearly revealed. For instance:

PROBLEM: If the mass of an electron is about 9×10^{-28} grams, and the mass of a proton is about 1.62×10^{-24} grams, about how many times the mass of an electron is the mass of a proton?

If you are hesitant about the operation to perform, make up numbers that are easier to grasp: Let the proton weigh 16 grams, and the electron 2 grams.

Obviously, the proton will weigh $\frac{16}{2} = 8$ times as much as the electron.

Hence the proton will weigh $\frac{1.62 \times 10^{-24}}{9 \times 10^{-28}} =$ about 1800 times as much as the electron.

3. Another effective technique, especially in word problems leading to equations, is to choose an answer *first* and from this to figure out the arithmetic procedure involved. For example:

PROBLEM: An alloy of copper and zinc is 10% zinc, the alloy weighing 400 lbs. How many pounds of pure zinc should be added to this alloy to make an alloy which is 20% zinc?

To discover the arithmetic procedure, let us add 100 lbs. of zinc. Then the new mixture of 500 lbs. contains the original 40 lbs. of zinc plus 100 lbs., or 140 lbs. The fraction of zinc is $\dfrac{140}{500}$, which reduces to $\dfrac{28}{100}$, or .28, or 28%. In our problem we do not know how much zinc to add, but we do know that the per cent of zinc is 20%. So, letting $x =$ no. of lbs. of zinc to be added,

$\dfrac{40 + x}{400 + x} = \dfrac{20}{100}.$ Compare this equation carefully with the arithmetic performed above.

Solving, $x = 50$ lbs.

Make use of the "educated guess."   Still another technique is the "educated guess" at the answer. When you are required in a problem to find the numerical value of some quantity, it is a good practice to guess at, or estimate, the answer in advance. A little slip in the mechanical work may cause a large error and give you an obviously absurd result, and the preliminary guess may enable you to catch and correct such an error. On the other hand, you may find that your guess is way off the mark; but through such experiences you may improve your mathematical intuition. All good scientists and mathematicians have to be good guessers, able to set up workable hypotheses out of their thorough knowledge of processes and calculations.

Check your results.   Get in the habit of checking your results by one or more of the following methods: (1) substitute your answer for the unknown in the problem, to see whether it agrees with the given information and satisfies the given conditions; (2) re-work the problem by an alternate method; (3) estimate the answer before attacking the problem, and use it as a measuring stick. Checking can reveal errors both of analysis and of computation, and it reinforces understanding. Checking is *not* a duplication of effort and a waste of time, but an important and constructive process.

Use short cuts.   Your efficiency in all mathematical operations will be improved if you are constantly alert for opportunities to use short cuts. For instance:

> PROBLEM: A chemical mixture calls for 2.5 cc of element A to every 5.5 cc of element B. If this is cut down to 1.5 cc of element A, how many cc of element B should be used?

The usual way of solving this problem in direct proportion is to let $b =$ no. of cc of element B. Then,

$$\frac{2.5}{1.5} = \frac{5.5}{b},$$

and by using the principle of a proportion, that the product of the first and fourth terms (extremes) equals the product of the second and third terms (means), we solve the equation:

$$2.5b = (1.5)(5.5),$$
$$b = \frac{(1.5)(5.5)}{(2.5)},$$
$$b = 3.3 \text{ cc.}$$

However, a more efficient procedure is to note that you "cut down" element A by a factor of $\frac{1.5}{2.5}$. Hence element B will be reduced by the same factor:

$$\frac{1.5}{2.5} \cdot 5.5 = 3.3 \text{ cc.}$$

Using short cuts also implies doing as much mental arithmetic as you can. Here are a few examples of calculations that you can easily do without resorting to pencil and paper.

To multiply a two-digit number by a one-digit number, such as 34×4:

$$(30 + 4)4 = (30)(4) + (4)(4) = 120 + 16 = 136.$$

To multiply a number by 25, divide it by 4 and multiply by 100 (i.e., append two zeros); for example, 25×32:

$$32 \div 4 = 8, \text{ with two zeros appended} = 800.$$

Here's another example. In evaluating a quantity such as

$$\frac{.00056 \times .25}{.00007},$$

take advantage of the fundamental principle that multiplying the numerator and the denominator of a fraction by a number (not zero) will not change the value of the fraction. In this case, multiply numerator and denominator by 100,000. Also, since $.25 = \frac{1}{4}$, the entire quantity reduces to $\frac{56 \times \frac{1}{4}}{7}$, or $8 \times \frac{1}{4} = 2$.

Learn to use the slide rule. A widely circulated item of student folklore is that the slide rule is only for engineers and scientists and is hard to use. This simply is not true, as junior high school students of average intelligence can and do demonstrate. Essentially, the slide rule is a device consisting of a fixed rule and a sliding one, both marked with graduated logarithmic scales. Calculations are made by suitably juxtaposing one scale against the other and reading the result. There are numerous models, ranging from simple ones on which relatively uncomplicated processes are computed, to elaborate ones for very complex and difficult processes. Unless you are planning to go on to advanced courses in the sciences or engineering, you should probably get one of the simpler and less expensive models, at least to start with. You will find it extremely useful in multiplication and division — and special cases of these, such as finding percentages, calculating ratios, raising to powers, extracting roots, and other time-consuming operations. Although at first, while you are learning to use it, you will find the slide rule less accurate and more time-consuming than computation "by hand," the tremendous saving of time that results when you have mastered it will far outweigh any temporary inconvenience.

THE PROPER ROLE OF MEMORY

In the study of mathematics most students rely entirely too much on memory. Competence in mathematics is not, to any great extent, a matter of remembering things. To take a very simple example, a child in the early grades memorizes his multiplication tables. This gives him a convenient mathematical tool and contributes to his speed in performing arithmetical operations. But it is much more important for him to see how these multiplication tables are made up by addition. Suppose he has forgotten the product 7 times 9. If he happens to know that 5 times 9 is 45, he can, by adding 9's quickly, deduce that 6 times 9 is 54 and 7 times 9 is 63. Or he may know that 10 times 7 is 70 and find, by subtracting 7, that 9 times 7 is 63. He should not be completely helpless when he has forgotten a particular product. This means, of course, that he should build up his own table for 9 times 1, 9 times 2, 9 times 3, etc., by adding 9's before he tries to memorize the results.

This kind of thing is important throughout the study of mathematics. Algebra students memorize the formula for solving a quadratic equation,

$$x = \frac{-b \pm \sqrt{b^2 - 4ac}}{2a}$$

But if they have not used the formula for several years, they have probably forgotten it. They may remember the general appearance of the formula but have forgotten, say, whether the sign under the radical is plus or minus. How can they now solve an equation such as $3x^2 - 10x + 2 = 0$? Memorizing the formula is a *convenience;* but an understanding of the process of completing the square, by which the formula is derived, is much more important. Students always seem to remember the formula $\sin^2 x + \cos^2 x = 1$, but they forget the similar formula connecting tan x and sec x. If they know the meaning of the trigonometric functions sin x, cos x, tan x, sec x (even for acute angles x), it is a trivial matter to recover these formulas when they have been forgotten. But some students who remember the formula $\sin^2 x + \cos^2 x = 1$ may be unable to show why this simple formula is true.

A practical reason why mathematical ability need not depend very largely on memory is that textbooks and handbooks are usually available in which to look up the forgotten rule or formula or number. One usually remembers that sin $30° = 1/2$, and it would be convenient if one could remember all the numerical values given in a table of sines of angles from $0°$ to $90°$. But it would clearly be foolish to attempt such a memory stunt. When you want a numerical value for sin 41°, you simply look it up in a table. True, if you have not studied calculus, you will have to accept the value of sin 41° on the authority of the table. So far as you can, however, you should learn the underlying processes and computations on which formulas and tables are based, rather than rely on memory or authority. This way, when memory fails or a textbook is not at hand, you will not be completely helpless: you can reconstruct the needed formula or value for yourself.

SKILLS ARE IMPORTANT — UNDERSTANDING IS ESSENTIAL

In the study of mathematics, then, there are two objectives: to develop skill and accuracy in certain formal processes, and to acquire a clear understanding of the meaning of these manipulations and the reasons for them. Too many students put all their effort into the first of these objectives. They learn rules and formulas, depending almost entirely on memory. This way is "right," that way is "wrong," with teacher or textbook being the authority for "right" and "wrong." Students too seldom ask *why* this is right or that is wrong. Following the rules that have been given them, they go through a process and obtain a correct result, but often have little understanding of the real meaning of the process or the result. The student in calculus can differentiate x^5, by rule, and obtain $5x^4$ as the derivative without any understanding of *why* he writes the 5 as a coefficient and reduces the exponent to 4, and without knowing what the derivative $5x^4$ means when he has obtained it. If one should memorize and reproduce correctly the sounds which constitute a sentence in the Russian language without knowing anything of their significance, he would not be speaking Russian — he would merely be making Russian noises. And if a student manipulates mathematical processes correctly without understanding their meaning, his work is not mathematics at all — he is merely making mathematical marks. The vast shorthand symbolism that has been invented to record and communicate mathematical ideas is only the *language* of mathematics, and language is a doubtful asset to anyone who has no ideas to communicate. It is, for example, a convenience to memorize the formula

$$\frac{d}{dx} x^m = mx^{m-1},$$

but this symbolism is *mathematics* only for the student who understands something of the meaning of a derivative and why this formula gives the derivative in this particular case.

PRECISION IN THE LANGUAGE OF MATHEMATICS

As you progress in mathematical insight and understanding, the language of mathematics becomes increasingly important. You must know the *exact* meaning of mathematical words and symbols: such words as "factor," "polynomial," "root," "slope," derivative," and "integral"; and such symbols as

$$+, =, (\,), \frac{d}{dx}, \int_a^b f(x)dx.$$

It would seem that the word "equal" and the corresponding symbol, $=$, are easy to understand, yet students will sometimes say that one equation is *equal* to another, or write

$$x + 1 = \frac{y}{2} =$$
$$2x + 2 = y.$$

The student who writes this possibly *means* something which is correct, but he *writes* something which is incorrect and does not express what he means. Such carelessness with the language of mathematics is not uncommon even among the better students. A student whose mathematical *thinking* is sound is often unable to *communicate* his ideas. When the instructor asks him a question, he may know the correct answer but give the wrong one because he uses the wrong words. Or he may misinterpret the words of the question and thus go astray.

Learn the language and symbolism of mathematics, and learn to use these words and symbols precisely. Only then can you fully and accurately communicate with others, orally or in writing, in the realm of mathematics.

Approaching the Natural Sciences*

Because of the role of science in modern life, you will find it of immense value to have the first-hand contact with scientific outlook and method which a course in one of the natural sciences[1] can give you. For science has its special and characteristic way of coming at knowledge, different from that of any other subject in the curriculum. It is not concerned with values, like literature; or with pastness, like history; or with logical system, like mathematics; or with mental and social processes, like the social sciences. It does not ask or seek to explain *why;* that is the province of philosophy and religion. Science is concerned with finding out *what* the facts of nature are and *how* natural processes work.

SCIENCE IS PROBLEM–SOLVING

The scientist works on the frontiers of the physical universe, where the known trails off into the unknown, and new knowledge is won by asking and answering questions that lend themselves to the collection of experimental data. His goal is not to make space ships or to find cures for human ills but to extend human understanding of the nature and operations of physical reality. He succeeds in his assault on the unknown not through isolated individual effort, but by building on the knowledge transmitted from past generations of scientific seekers, and by sharing knowledge with his contemporaries.

In a first course, it may seem to you that the study of science consists largely in absorbing great amounts of factual information. But this is only because you are at the beginning. Your textbook is in effect a record or summary of the present state of information in the field; it is a means by which you can stand on the shoulders of the past in order to survey the present and even peer into the future. The true concern of science is not with amassing a body of fact for its own sake, but with identifying and

---

* Adapted in part from material supplied by Kenneth Greisen.
[1] Physics, chemistry, astronomy, geology, biology, botany, and zoology (together with subdivisions and combinations of these, such as physiology, cytology, genetics, biochemistry, etc.).

solving problems along the frontiers of knowledge — problems for which the answers are not yet known and the questions are hardly yet shaped.

Hence scientific activity does not center in the study of books, documents, and records such as you are used to in your other courses; it is focused in the laboratory where the problems are formulated and attacked. Here, in the laboratory, you will learn to practice the experimental techniques that have made modern problem-solving science possible. You will not be pushing back any frontiers in an introductory course, but you will gain insight into the scientific method that enables practicing scientists and advanced students to do so.

THE SCIENTIFIC METHOD

A natural science begins with observation. In some sciences, such as geology and biology, some observation can profitably be done in the field. But the most valuable and precise observations are made in the laboratory, where all factors of a selected situation from nature can be controlled. This makes it possible to experiment by reproducing a situation any number of times and varying any of the factors at will.

The experiment of the single variable is the keystone to the scientific method of problem-solving. First, from observation and speculation, comes identification of the problem. Experimental data relating to it are collected; and from an analysis of these, a hypothesis (tentative solution) is then set up — an inclusive pattern which appears to account for most or all of the data. Now the hypothesis is tested again and again by experiment, and eventually is verified, modified (and re-tested), or given up as unworkable. If verified, the hypothesis, or theory, provides a blueprint for predicting, and sometimes controlling, natural processes.

SCIENCE IS QUANTITATIVE

Science is quantitative but never exact. The "facts" of science, being established on observation and experiment, within the framework of hypotheses, are not absolute and final truths; they simply represent the best description and analysis of the physical universe that scientists have been able to make up to any given time. If new findings disprove an accepted hypothesis or fact, the scientist must be prepared to discard it. Not so long ago it was a "fact" of science that the atom was indivisible; today nuclear physics is based on the "fact" that the atom can be split. Estimates of the sizes and distances of stars are frequently revised as experimental techniques are improved and refined. The scientist does not become emotionally attached to hypotheses or facts, or convert them into values.

All measurements, of course, have limited accuracy. An ever-present question, therefore, is the degree of accuracy that may be expected. Equally important, what is a significant deviation between an actual measurement and that predicted by the hypothesis? Science, you can see, requires a refined concept of precision — not perfect accuracy, but meticulous care and an understanding of the limits of probable error. In your laboratory work, pay serious attention to measurements, and to estimating and reporting errors in them.

THE NEED FOR PRECISION IN LANGUAGE

Science is always struggling with the need for precise definition of terms. Most English words have many different meanings, depending on the context in which they are used. But in scientific usage it is unsatisfactory to rely on context for meaning. If ambiguity and error in communication are to be avoided, terms must have fixed, consistent meanings and must be defined as completely as possible. Yet even some of the fundamental conceptual terms (e.g., time, mass, force, size, color, life, death, plant, animal) are still subject to dispute. As science advances, these and other complicated terms (e.g., life, cell, virus, gene, molecule, atom, nucleus, elementary particle, crystal, galaxy), which began as vague and tentative concepts, are progressively acquiring richer and more definite meanings. Meanwhile, continuing observations lead to the emergence of new crude concepts to be refined and delimited in the future. Inevitably scientists in the forefront of research have to make use of some tentative concepts and hence some ill-defined words.

HOW TO READ A TEXTBOOK IN SCIENCE

Your textbook represents an essential body of factual information which you need as background to the main business of a science, which is problem-solving in laboratory experimentation. There are a few special things to keep in mind in reading scientific materials.

First, you will need to develop the ability to visualize and manipulate mentally as you read. Much scientific writing consists in descriptions of structures, models, operations, and procedures, and your understanding will depend largely on the degree to which you can "see" these in your mind. Fortunately, most textbooks and articles in science are heavily illustrated with diagrams and pictures to give you visual help in reading. Learn to use illustrations and text to supplement one another.

In the second place, you will find that your science textbooks are crowded with terms that are new to you. Since these terms stand for essential concepts, you must know precisely what they mean if you are to understand the subject matter. Again the textbook writers will have anticipated your need and provided help. The important new terms are usually emphasized by italic or heavy type at their first occurrence, and specifically defined at that point or in a glossary at the end of the book. Put extra time and attention on memorizing these terms and learning what they mean.

Third, learn the language of scientific measurement: the metric system of weights and measures, and the Centigrade as well as the Fahrenheit temperature scale. Learn to think meaningfully in these quantities and measures, so that you will not be reading mere words and symbols.

Finally, don't skip over the problems. "I understand the subject but just can't do the problems" is a self-contradictory remark. If you really understand the material, you can work the accompanying problems. Difficulty with problems is a sure sign that you are hazy on basic principles, or weak in the mathematical background you are assumed to have, or both.

Different sciences call for different attacks and emphases in the reading. In a general way we may say, for example, that biology and geology place relatively heavy emphasis on key terms and definitions; physics and astronomy, on measurement and mathematics; biology and chemistry, on manipulation; physics and chemistry, on visualization.

IN THE LABORATORY

Keep in mind that the laboratory is the front line and that the techniques of problem-solving, which you are learning on a modest scale, are the same as those that achieve the great break-throughs in science. Here are some hints on good attitudes and habits for laboratory work:

1. Be painstaking and accurate in observing and recording data. Write down everything you think may be pertinent. Some things seem so obvious at the time that you may be tempted to think there is no point in recording them; but memory fades, and without a complete record you may be unable to recall important items of information: identification and properties of equipment, ranges and units of measuring instruments, dimensions and schematic diagram of apparatus, sensitivity of a balance, headings and units for columns of data, quirks in the performance of equipment, and numerous other details.

2. Follow the practice of professional scientists in keeping a full record of all your calculations, observations, and results in a special notebook; don't ever write anything down on separate scraps of paper — not even your arithmetical calculations. If you make mistakes, cross them out and go on from there, but keep everything as part of your complete record. Start your record of each experiment or laboratory session on a new page, headed with the date. In this way you will have a permanent log of all your data and mental processes pertaining to any problem on which you have worked — all the raw materials for your final report.

3. Organize the recording of data. Arrange them so that they will be clear and fully labeled for later reference. The few extra minutes you take to make neat and orderly records during the laboratory period will save you time that you would otherwise have to spend later in deciphering and arranging haphazard notes.

4. Baby the apparatus. Treat it tenderly, and coax out of it the best

performance of which it is capable. Make a note of its limitations and the expected accuracy of the measurements. No real equipment is quite like the ideal version pictured in a textbook or laboratory manual.

5. Don't put too much trust in either yourself or the apparatus. Carry out at least an approximate analysis (including rough graphs) of the data while you are taking them, so that you can detect anything that is going wrong, either through your fault or that of the apparatus. In this way you may have a chance to remedy the situation in time to save the experiment — perhaps by readjusting the apparatus, checking or repeating a step, or asking your instructor for advice and aid.

6. Keep in mind the purpose of the laboratory work in which you are engaged. This will save you from wandering off the track and wasting time and effort.

7. Write up your reports clearly, legibly, and concisely, and in the prescribed form. The style should be impersonal; in technical reports it is customary to use the passive voice, more than in other writing, to avoid saying "I." The conventional form of a laboratory report, with minor variations, is approximately as follows:

Purpose (Object): A thesis statement to explain what the problem is.

Theory: The background for the problem and the justification for your method of attack.

Apparatus (Equipment, Materials): A listing and brief description of essentials, often including a sketch of the apparatus.

Procedure: A step-by-step report of what you did.

Results: A step-by-step record of your observations.

Conclusion: A summary of your findings and an assessment of their accuracy to show how they succeed or fail in resolving the problem with which you started.

Above all, in writing a report, remember that your purpose is to make your findings understandable to a reader; that the principles of good written communication are not something to be relegated to a pigeon-hole labeled "English courses" but are among the most essential tools of today's scientist.

17

Living Realistically

Without good emotional health, academic and social success is difficult, if not impossible. A student lacking emotional stability finds great difficulty in studying and learning. He wastes time worrying, is unable to complete his homework, and then worries more about what he has left undone. He also has trouble getting along with people, is generally suspicious of them, and harbors deep feelings of inadequacy and self-doubt.

To derive greater benefit from the principles and techniques presented in this book, and to pave the way for a happier future, try to maintain or improve your emotional health by practicing the following eleven principles set forth by the National Association for Mental Health.*

Talk It Out. When something worries you, talk it out; don't bottle it up. Confide your worry to some level-headed person you can trust: a good friend, your father or mother, your clergyman, doctor, faculty adviser, counselor, or dean. Talking things out helps to relieve strain, helps you see your worry in a clearer light, and often helps you see what you can do about it.

Escape for a While. When things go wrong, it is sometimes helpful to get away from the problem for a while, to lose yourself in a movie, a book, a game, or a brief trip. Making yourself stand there and suffer can be a form of self-punishment, not a way to solve a problem. It is perfectly realistic and healthy to escape long enough to recover breath and balance. But be prepared to come back and deal with your difficulty when you are more composed, and when you and others involved are in better condition emotionally and mentally to deal with it.

Work Off Your Anger. If you find yourself using anger as a general pattern of behavior, remember that while anger may give you a temporary

* The following material on the "eleven things you can do" is reprinted with slight adaptations from *How to Deal with Your Tensions* (© National Association for Mental Health, 1957), written by Dr. George S. Stevenson, National and International Consultant, National Association for Mental Health, in collaboration with Harry Milt, Director of Public Relations of the National Association for Mental Health. Used by permission.

sense of righteousness, or even of power, it will generally leave you feeling foolish and sorry in the end. If you feel like lashing out at someone who has provoked you, try holding off that impulse for a while. Let it wait until tomorrow. Meanwhile, direct your pent-up energy into other channels. Pitch into some physical activity like athletics, cleaning your room, or taking a long walk. Working the anger out of your system and cooling it off for a day or two will leave you much better prepared to handle your problem intelligently and constructively.

Give In Occasionally. If you find yourself getting into frequent quarrels, and feeling obstinate and defiant, remember that that's the way frustrated children behave. Try to understand the basic reason for frustration. Stand your ground on what you believe is right, but do so calmly and make allowance for the fact that you *could* be wrong. Even if you're dead right, it's easier on your system to give in once in a while on matters that are not fundamentally important. If you yield some ground, you'll usually find that others will too. At least, you can "agree to disagree." The result will be relief from tension, the achievement of a practical solution, and a satisfying sense of maturity.

Do Something for Others. If you spend a good deal of time worrying about yourself, try doing something for somebody else. You'll find that this takes the steam out of your own worries and — even better — gives you a fine feeling of having done something worthwhile.

Take One Thing at a Time. For people under tension, an ordinary work load can seem unbearable. The load looks so great that it becomes painful to tackle any part of it. Remember that this is a temporary condition. You can work your way out of it by tackling a few of the most urgent tasks one at a time, setting aside all the rest for the time being. Once you dispose of these obstacles, you'll see that the rest are not insurmountable either. You'll be in a mood to accomplish more, and the rest of the tasks will go more easily. If you feel you can't set anything aside and must do everything at once, reflect: are you sure you aren't overestimating the importance of the things you do — that is, your own importance?

Shun the "Superman" Urge. Some people expect too much from themselves and are in a constant state of worry and anxiety because they think they are not achieving as much as they should. They try for perfection in everything. Admirable as this ideal is, it is an invitation to failure, for no one can be perfect in everything. Decide which things you do well (usually they are the things you like best to do and are most important to you), and put your major effort into these. As for the things you can't do so well, give them the best of your effort and ability, but don't take yourself to task if you can't achieve top honors or break records.

Go Easy with Your Criticism. Some people expect too much of others, and feel frustrated, let down, disappointed, even betrayed, when another person does not measure up to those expectations. Each person has his own virtues, his own shortcomings, his own values, his own right to develop as an individual. We are being unfair to him when we try to fit him into a preconceived pattern, or attempt to make him over to suit ourselves. If you find much to criticize in another person, perhaps you are holding him to a standard which you would like to attain yourself. Instead of being critical of him, search out his good points and encourage him to develop them. This will give both of you satisfaction and help you gain a better perspective on yourself.

Give the Other Fellow a Break. When you are under emotional tension, you may feel that you have to "get there first" — to edge out the other person, even if the goal is as trivial as getting ahead on the highway. Everything becomes a race, and somebody is bound to get hurt, either physically, as on the highway, or emotionally and mentally in the endeavor to live a full life. It need not be this way; competition is contagious, but so is cooperation. When you give the other fellow a break, you often make things easier for yourself. If he no longer feels you are a threat to him, he stops being a threat to you.

Make Yourself Available. Many of us have the feeling that we are being left out, neglected, rejected. Often we just imagine that others are slighting us, when in reality they are eager for us to make the first move. Instead of shrinking away and withdrawing, it is healthier and more practical to keep yourself available and to make some of the overtures instead of always waiting to be asked. Of course, it is equally a mistake to push yourself forward on every occasion. This is often misinterpreted and may lead to real rejection. There is a middle ground between withdrawing and pushing. Try it.

Schedule Your Recreation. Many people drive themselves so hard that they allow themselves too little time for recreation — an essential for good physical, mental, and emotional health. They find it hard to take time out. Such people are helped by a fixed schedule allocating definite hours when they are to engage in some form of recreation. And almost everyone will benefit from a hobby or absorbing interest to which he can turn with pleasure in off hours for a change of pace from his regular work.

No stage of life is free from problems, not even the "golden college years" which forgetful alumni recall as untroubled and idyllic. Nor should one wish it otherwise; for life by very definition involves growth and change and decision-making and adjustment, sometimes pleasant, sometimes painful. What makes the college years unique is not their freedom from human problems, but the unparalleled opportunity they offer you, at the outset of your adult life, to devote your full energies to becoming the person you want to be. Most students recognize and appreciate the opportunity for intellectual development, and this book has been largely concerned with helping you make the most of it. But, as we have also tried to suggest, the maintenance of a sense of balance and order in living — a healthy emotional climate — is essential in the cultivation of good study habits. Daily life itself has been termed an effective therapy; and it is through living each day realistically that you can best maintain your emotional health and hence the more readily achieve your academic goal.

Index